Praise for *Ready-to-Go Instruct Collaboration, Communicatic*

"This book provides tools and strategies that will help educators become more reflective of their teaching practices while helping students take control of their learning."

—*Ellen Asregadoo, Teacher*
PS 190
New York City, NY

"These two ladies are truly "teachers' teachers" and have gifted the profession with a plethora of proven, research-based strategies to make learning more powerful and teaching more fun! The book is arranged in such a way that it can be read as a whole or used as a quick and easy resource to improve instruction in a certain area. Strategies are presented in an easy-to-follow format, and suggestions for use in different content areas and for a variety of ages are given. This book is beneficial for individual teacher use or could be incorporated into small group or whole staff professional development. It is obvious that White and Braddy have experience with learners of all ages, including teachers. This is a valuable resource to make even the best teacher better!"

—*Ellen Auchenpaugh, Academic Coach*
Cobb County School District
Austell, GA

"In today's age of instant gratification and the fast-paced world of information overload, this is the exact book that teachers, administrators, and university professors need to create a learning environment that fosters high levels of engagement and culture-building in one's classroom, school, or district. White and Braddy, master teachers and coaches, hit the nail on the head with their first book, which provides ready-to-use strategies that build a classroom of highly engaged learners.

What makes their book unique is not only the vignettes that are created for each chapter, but also the "Why It Works" sections. The brain is a pattern-seeking device, and when we can place meaning in why we do what we do, we are able to better preserve the integrity, intentionality, and fidelity of the strategy. Educators have to engage students in developing episodic memories that enhance the learning to move it from short- to long-term memory.

I've highlighted, sticky-noted, and written in every margin my own ideas and suggestions for my university classes and presentations at a recent principal conference, and even shared them with my wife, who is a high school administrator. This is more than a handbook—it's a life-changing teacher resource for the new or skilled teacher. As you lesson plan, keep this text beside you to enhance your ability to have students dig deeper in the content, push and support them to develop analytic thinking, and, most important, prepare them for tomorrow's world.

The only professional support that is better than *Ready-to-Go Instructional Strategies That Build Collaboration, Communication, and Critical Thinking* is to have Denise White and Alisa Braddy in your own classroom or school coaching you. Trust me. I know."

—*Dr. Adam D. Drummond, Educational Consultant*
Drummond Educational Innovations
Huntington, IN

"This book is a dream come true for educators—teachers, instructional coaches, and administrators! It is an all-in-one resource filled with tools that engage learners at all levels and with diverse learning styles.

It is so user-friendly and organized just like a lesson for easy implementation of new strategies. Chapter 1 begins with hooking the learners through anticipatory set and continues unraveling many strategies while providing reflection and ways to increase the rigor of instruction and student learning. Collaboration, critical thinking, and communication drive the instructional strategies that create student-centered learning. The final chapter focuses on engaging lesson closure with strategies that drive home and affirm the learning.

This is truly a masterpiece that builds the educator's toolbox with ready-to-use strategies! The entire book or selected portions can easily be used for professional development or while coaching teachers in student-centered instruction.

White and Braddy have utilized their personal classroom experiences as well as sound research in crafting this resource. *Ready-to-Go Instructional Strategies That Build Collaboration, Communication, and Critical Thinking* provides a plethora of 21st century best teaching practices!"

—*Janet M. Fickling, Principal*
Midway Elementary
Lexington, SC

"Never in my professional reading have I found a book to be so practically written and useful! Although the strategies are all based in research, you never feel talked down to or confused. Actually, it's the opposite, you can almost feel White and Braddy's presence, as if they are right there, speaking to you, giving suggestions that will have immediate impact."

—*Sarah Hadden, Director of Curriculum and Technology*
Greenwood Lake UFSD
Monroe, NY

"This is a must-read for teachers, administrators, and curriculum leaders! It is filled with exciting yet practical ideas and strategies to actively engage students in learning while challenging and encouraging critical thinking at the same time. The organization of the book is so user-friendly. From believable vignettes to understandable definitions to explanations of why it works to practical strategies, this is a truly practical guide for anyone who teaches. It will resonate with all educators and draw them in with its brilliant yet timeless ideas and strategies."

—*Donna Hooks, Retired Principal*
Georgetown, SC

"White and Braddy provide a treasure trove of practical, proven, and powerful strategies that outline a road map to meaningful student engagement. *Ready-to-Go Instructional Strategies That Build Collaboration, Communication, and Critical Thinking* is an easy-to-use resource for educators who wish to find new ways to work with today's youth. This book is sure to bring growth and new learning for educators both young and old."

—*Tom Padalino, Principal*
Thoreau Demonstration Academy
Tulsa, OK

"Finally we will be able to clean out our bookshelves of educational reference books and replace them with *Ready-to-Go Instructional Strategies That Build Collaboration, Communication, and Critical Thinking*! This is an easy-to-use, quick guide containing numerous instructional strategies. Whether you're a veteran teacher or new to the profession, *Ready-to-Go Instructional Strategies* will help you build collaboration, communication, and critical thinking. For veterans, it's a one-stop collection of tried and true strategies with quick reminders of how and why to use them. For those new to the profession, it will quickly become the best support you've ever encountered! I love recommending this treasure to the educators with whom I work!"

—*Brenda Russell, Instructional Coach*
Cocoa Beach, FL

"I love that the strategies in this book are listed with explanations and actual examples of setting them up. It is great for both new and seasoned teachers–it either confirms work they are doing or gives/refreshes new ideas to use and when they can be used."

—*Debra A. Scarpelli, Math Educator/ESL*
Pawtucket School Dept./RIMLE
Pawtucket, RI

"Denise White and Alisa Braddy hit a home run with this well-written work. Educators will come to treasure this impressive toolkit as a one-stop reference to design and deliver engaging and rigorous instruction. The use of scenarios conveys an excellent model of real-world situations teachers may encounter in the classroom. The authors' step-by-step strategies offer job-embedded active learning for teachers in their daily practice. Add all of this up and you have a model of how teachers can effectively make the switch from planning for teaching to planning for learning. I will ensure that this book is in the hands of our teachers and other instructional leaders as a road map for providing engaging, rigorous, and relevant learning in our district."

—*Lowell H. Strike, PhD, Superintendent of Schools*
Little Elm ISD
Little Elm, TX

READY-TO-GO
INSTRUCTIONAL STRATEGIES THAT BUILD
COLLABORATION, COMMUNICATION, & CRITICAL THINKING

READY-TO-GO
INSTRUCTIONAL STRATEGIES THAT BUILD
COLLABORATION, COMMUNICATION, & CRITICAL THINKING

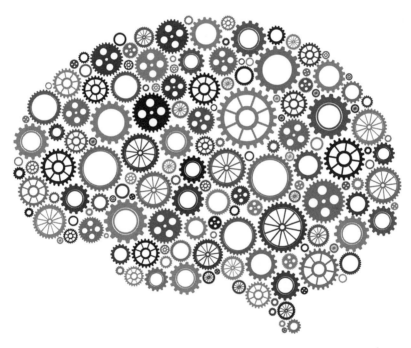

DENISE WHITE
ALISA BRADDY

CORWIN
A SAGE Publishing Company

FOR INFORMATION:

Corwin

A SAGE Company

2455 Teller Road

Thousand Oaks, California 91320

(800) 233-9936

www.corwin.com

SAGE Publications Ltd.

1 Oliver's Yard

55 City Road

London EC1Y 1SP

United Kingdom

SAGE Publications India Pvt. Ltd.

B 1/I 1 Mohan Cooperative Industrial Area

Mathura Road, New Delhi 110 044

India

SAGE Publications Asia-Pacific Pte. Ltd.

3 Church Street

#10-04 Samsung Hub

Singapore 049483

Program Director: Jessica Allan

Senior Associate Editor: Kimberly Greenberg

Editorial Assistant: Katie Crilley

Production Editor: Amy Schroller

Copy Editor: Terri Lee Paulsen

Typesetter: Hurix Systems Pvt. Ltd.

Proofreader: Dennis W. Webb

Indexer: Judy Hunt

Cover Designer: Anupama Krishnan

Marketing Manager: Jill Margulies

Printed in the United States of America

ISBN 978-1-5063-3395-3

This book is printed on acid-free paper.

MIX
Paper from
responsible sources
FSC® C012947

17 18 19 20 21 10 9 8 7 6 5 4 3 2 1

Contents

Preface

CREATING THIS BOOK

As education consultants, we have been delivering professional development for many, many years, and after every presentation, training, or instructional coaching session, someone will approach us and ask, "Is there a book where I can find all the instructional strategies you used?" Our answer is always vague: "Well, we get our ideas from lots of different places . . ." The response was nearly always, "You two should write a book so that we could find them all in one place. That would help so much."

It is also common for teachers we work with to call us or e-mail us asking for ideas for strategies to make lessons more engaging. One middle school teacher, who is also a dear friend, would call about once a month asking for specific strategies to make her lessons more student-centered. Each time, she would remind us that she would not call us so much if we had a book to give her. Wendy was very specific in what she wanted: "It needs to be easy to use. I want to be able to turn to a strategy and have it explained step by step. I also want it to have a chart listing all the strategies and what they are good for." Great ideas! Someone should write a book like that!

Alisa wanted it to be us, and kept pushing for us to get to work on a book. Denise was resistant, however, wondering how we could possibly fit one more thing into our busy lives. Then, one night at dinner with her family at a Chinese restaurant, Denise broke open a fortune cookie and read the message inside: "You are a lover of words. You should write a book." Who could argue with that? So we carved out some time the next month, dove in, and started writing. Anytime we felt like giving up, we would remind each other of all the teachers, administrators, and instructional coaches who have asked us for this book. And we kept writing. For them.

HOW TO USE THIS BOOK

Teachers

There is no right or wrong way to use this book. It is meant to be a handbook and a toolkit for you to use as you plan for student learning, not a text to be read from cover to cover. There are reflection questions at the end of each chapter to challenge your thinking and push you to take action. The strategies in each chapter can be used to design lessons from scratch or to enhance even the most scripted program.

There are lots of places to start. You may want to read through the vignettes first. All the scenarios have been taken from either our own classroom experiences or from the teachers and students we have worked with across the country. If you see yourself or one of your students in one of them, check out the strategies that worked for that teacher. Maybe they will work for you, too.

Another starting point is the matrix. If you know there are elements you want to add to your lessons, such as academic conversation and movement, trace those elements through the matrix and find the strategies that include them. These strategies can be put into any lesson, any grade level, any content. You could also dig into the chapters that address those elements to discover what they include and why they are effective.

You could also start with the strategies themselves. Glance through the Contents and find a strategy that sounds interesting. Check out the time needed and the preparation required. The procedures are right there for you to put onto a slide or write on the board to guide your students through the process.

Administrators

You can use this book as a resource as you work with your teachers. If you want a teacher to let her students work together more often, you can give her a specific strategy from the collaboration chapter to try. If this teacher tells you that she has tried group work but it just doesn't work with these kids, you can give her the sections that describe what collaboration is and why it works.

You could also use this for a book study during staff meetings or professional learning communities (PLCs). The reflection questions at the end of each chapter lend themselves to rich and meaningful discussions during PLCs. You could also divide the chapters up between grade levels or departments or among the members of a PLC and let them take the lead in modeling the strategies and explaining the research behind them.

Instructional Coaches

You can use these strategies as you plan presentations for teachers. Allow participants to process the content you are teaching through an instructional strategy that they can also take away and add to their toolkits.

When you coach teachers, you can use the research to help them understand why adding a certain element like reflection and closure to their lessons addresses the way the human brain learns. You can then offer specific strategies that they can try the next day.

You can also use this book as a coaching tool. Allow teachers to select an area they would like to focus on (anticipatory sets, movement, questioning, etc.) and use that chapter as a guide to talk about it, plan for it, and practice it. Use the reflection questions at the end of each chapter as springboards for discussion and ways to take action.

Suggestions

However you choose to use this book, here are some suggestions to optimize its effectiveness:

1. **Try a strategy more than once.** The first time is a new experience for both you and the students. It is an opportunity to analyze what went well and what didn't and to adjust the procedures for the next attempt.

2. **Try "hard" strategies in the safest environment.** If you are reticent to try a strategy because you don't know how it will go, try it first with your least challenging class or in your favorite content area. This will give you the best opportunity to experience the strategy and "work out the kinks" before implementing it with more challenging students or content.

3. **Collaborate with your colleagues.** Everyone brings a unique perspective to the table. If several of you try the same strategy, you can debrief it afterward and compare and contrast your experiences. You could also divide up several strategies and each of you be responsible for trying one and reporting back to the group how it went and what changes you would recommend.

4. **Mark up your book.** Remember, this is a handbook and a toolkit. Make it yours. Jot notes about what worked and what didn't. Note any adaptations you made or want to consider in the future.

Acknowledgments

How do you ever say thank you to everyone who had a hand in this journey?

A big shout-out to all the teachers and administrators we've met along the way who encouraged us to write this book and cheered us on throughout the process. We did this for you!

A huge hug to all the teachers who shared with us ways you have used these strategies in your own classrooms! Your examples made the chapters come to life.

All these ideas would have never made it from our brains onto these pages without our wonderful editor Jessica Allan, who walked beside us and held our hands through this whole process.

We are forever grateful to Corwin for giving these "green" writers the chance to be published authors.

Thank you to our families, who ate a lot of delivery pizza and take-out Chinese while we were tucked away on writing retreats. Now that we are finished, it doesn't mean we will start cooking, but we can't wait to share an egg roll with you.

Above all, we give thanks to God for the grace and strength to accomplish more than we thought possible.

PUBLISHER'S ACKNOWLEDGMENTS

Corwin gratefully acknowledges the contributions of the following reviewers:

Ellen Asregadoo
Teacher
PS 190
Brooklyn, NY

Jennifer Harper
Grade 4 Teacher & 2006 Vermont Teacher of the Year
Cavendish Town Elementary School
Proctorsville, VT

Debra A. Scarpelli
Math Educator/ESL
Pawtucket School Dept./RIMLE
Pawtucket, RI

Robert Wallon
Research Assistant and Graduate Student in Curriculum and Instruction
University of Illinois at Urbana–Champaign
Champaign, IL

About the Authors

Denise White taught at both the elementary and secondary levels for many years before working with adults in an instructional coaching capacity. She is currently working with teachers around the country as an education consultant. Denise lives in Tulsa, Oklahoma, with her husband and twin sons and can often be spotted riding her pink bike by the river.

Alisa H. Braddy is a former primary, elementary, and high school teacher with more than two decades of teaching experience. Alisa was a literacy specialist and instructional coach before she left to dedicate her full-time attention to educational consulting. She makes her home in Florence, South Carolina, with her husband, son, and a whole zoo full of animals.

Inspire and Engage Consulting Services is a full-service company specializing in customized professional development to improve teacher effectiveness and increase student achievement. Our common-sense approach to professional development is differentiated and relevant to every teacher we work with. Just like in our book, we offer strategies and resources that can be implemented immediately.

Find out more at our website: www.inspireandengage.com, and "like" the Inspire and Engage Consulting Services Facebook page to see where we have been and what we are doing.

To Mike—who believed this was possible long before I did.
This is for you. Keep pushing me to dream big.

—dw

To Mr. Spencer, my seventh-grade teacher—you know why.

—ahb

1 Hooking Them In

Powerful Strategies for Opening a Lesson

VIGNETTES

A Teacher's Perspective

Steve Gerald finished taking attendance and asked his third graders to take out their science journals. He was anxious to continue the lively discussion that had begun during yesterday's lesson on animal adaptations. He threw out a couple of questions with little response from students. "Guys, we just talked about this yesterday. What's going on? Is everyone still asleep this morning?" he asked in frustration. "Mr. Gerald, can we watch that animal video you showed yesterday?" asked LaTasha. "It was so cool!" Of course, the rest of the students began chiming in their support. That was yesterday's lesson! Why do they want to repeat what they've already done? Mr. Gerald was thinking about the great lesson he had planned for today . . . if only his students would get into it.

A Student's Perspective

LaTasha skipped into class. She couldn't wait to learn more about what animals do to survive. Yesterday they had seen the coolest video clip showing all the amazing things animals do. She hadn't wanted that lesson to end. Today Mr. Gerald asked them to get their notebooks and started asking some questions. LaTasha felt lost . . . where was he going with this? She thought maybe if they watched the video again it would help her answer his questions, but when she suggested this, Mr. Gerald just seemed to get frustrated. LaTasha just felt confused.

WHAT IS AN ANTICIPATORY SET?

Mr. Gerald can't wait to jump back in to his lesson, but his students aren't jumping with him. Are they just sleepy like Mr. Gerald thinks, or is there more to it? What was different about the previous day's lesson that led to such an engaging discussion?

The difference is simple but significant: the previous day the students were mentally prepared to absorb and process new content. The short video clip Mr. Gerald showed provided an anticipatory set, drawing the students in to the lesson and mentally preparing them for new learning. It allowed them to access their prior knowledge about the topic while also piquing their curiosity. They began constructing questions that they would seek to answer during the lesson. In short, within the first five to seven minutes of class, the students were hungry for what Mr. Gerald would teach them.

The anticipatory set only takes five to 10 minutes, but it is a crucial part of the lesson cycle because it serves as the "hook." It creates anticipation for the learning and primes the brain for taking in and processing information. A well-constructed anticipatory set creates a mental advanced organizer in the students' minds that gives them a place to file and organize the new information as it is taught.

Using a brief video clip, like Mr. Gerald did, is just one way to put the students' brains in a receptive state. This chapter will explore eight strategies for mentally engaging students in the content to be learned.

WHY IT WORKS

So it's a standard part of a classic lesson plan. But does it work? If an effort has been made to add an anticipatory set to a lesson, will students actually learn more? The research says yes. Although it has been examined under a few different names (anticipatory set, the emotional "hook," set of induction, advance organizers), a number of studies over the past several decades support its use in daily lessons.

Research is now confirming that, for lessons to produce desired learning results, students must initially feel passion and emotion about what they are learning. If the information perceived fails to elicit a positive emotional response, it will fail to be perceived as meaningful and will therefore have little chance of being selected into long-term memory banks (Wilson, 2015). This information is what stands out so we can focus upon it, organize it, and remember it. Study after study confirms that the more emotionality evoked, the easier it is to remember. A pioneering leader in defining emotional circuitry, Joseph LeDoux, notes, "Emotions, in short, amplify memory" (1998).

So what evokes emotionality? When anything is perceived as unusual, novel, accesses prior knowledge, and generates curiosity, norepinephrine is released to wake up the emotional center of the brain. This reaction allows for higher levels of mental awareness and arousal, attention, and focus, thereby creating intrinsic motivation and curiosity to ensure deeper understanding of content. Why? Exciting, interesting, and thought-provoking situations and events are better remembered than boring or neutral ones (Sprenger, 2005). This heightened state of hungering for knowledge, when students are magnetized by a new idea or a new situation and are compelled to explore more deeply, is why LaTasha was feeling so energetic, motivated, and curious during Mr. Gerald's first lesson and was so disappointed when the next day's lesson began so humdrum.

If emotions organize brain activity and drive attention and perception, then our daily lessons should include anticipatory sets that unlock our students' motivation, curiosity, and attention. By designing lessons that channel this energy toward the content being taught, students' everyday experiences in school will become more memorable and these concepts will move into long-term memory storage.

In the end, anticipatory sets evoke emotions that strongly influence our attention, help us make meaning of our experiences, and imprint strong memories in our brain (Wolfe, 2010).

STRATEGIES FOR ANTICIPATORY SETS

INSTRUCTIONAL VIDEO CLIPS

On Day 1, Mr. Gerald knew using an instructional video clip was a powerful tool for meaningful learning because it piqued interest and stimulated critical-thinking skills through active opportunities for students to generate their own questions. This is why LaTasha was skipping into his class the following day. She was excitedly awaiting the return of the video clip.

When instructional video clips are used as anticipatory sets, students make new connections between curriculum topics, and discover links between these topics and the world outside the classroom. Video clips can be used in a variety of meaningful ways: to illustrate complex concepts, show experiments that cannot be done in class, help hesitant learners become more task-focused, engage students in problem-solving and investigative activities, and provide shared learning experiences for all students.

On Day 2 of Mr. Gerald's lesson, he could have enhanced his lesson by implementing another video clip and attaching a specific learning task that connected to the essential information he wanted them to gain as part of his science objective for the lesson. This would give students a very specific purpose for watching and listening, and help springboard the lesson into deeper and richer discussions and processes. For example, if Mr. Gerald used the science standard that asked students to describe animal adaptations, then students could watch the video clip at the beginning of his lesson and complete a learning task that asked them to determine and describe one or more of the animal adaptations seen. Then after viewing, students could participate in productive academic discussions about the information found.

The Internet is replete with resources that teachers can use to find high-quality instructional video clips on virtually any topic. Listed below are a few that teachers have found to be especially helpful:

- www.khanacademy.org
- Disney Educational Productions: http://dep.disney.go.com
- teachertube.com
- http://www.watchknowlearn.org
- www.teachingchannel.org
- www.schooltube.com

Classroom Close-Up: Video Clips

After designing and constructing model roller coasters, I wanted my Gifted and Talented students to use advertising techniques effectively to promote their structures. To engage them in this part of the lesson, I used video clips of a variety of commercials. Before showing them each commercial, I asked them to think about what technique was being used to capture their attention and make them want to buy or use the product or service advertised. I showed each commercial twice: the first time just to give them the gist of the message, and the second time so they could truly analyze the technique being used and capture their thinking on a sticky note. After the second viewing, students discussed the technique and evidence from the commercial in small groups. These discussions provided the perfect springboard for my lesson on persuasion and created a catalyst for students to think about the most effective technique for their own advertisements.

—Tara Gordon, middle-school Gifted and Talented teacher, Tulsa, OK

Instructional Video Clips

Preparation: Choosing and viewing the video clip ahead of time is critical to ensure it correlates concisely with the standards, goals, and objectives for the topic being studied. A meaningful question/prompt should be developed ahead of time, as well, so students have something meaningful to attend to as they view the video clip.

Time Needed: 3–4 minutes

Grouping: Individuals, partners

Procedures for Students:

1. Listen to and watch the video clip.

2. Using today's "Purpose for Watching" prompt/question, find evidence in the video to answer.

3. Write (draw, discuss) answers using the provided graphic organizer.

4. Share your findings with a learning partner.

Suggested Adaptations and Applications to Other Content Areas:

- Very young students can participate in discussion pairs to successfully complete the learning tasks associated with the viewing of video clips.

- If the video clip is too long for one lesson, chunk it so students receive 2–3 minutes of it per lesson.

- If there is limited technology, set up a video station (with an iPad, laptop, etc.) and allow students to rotate through as they listen and watch. The same purpose for watching could be utilized, but the format for gaining the information will "look" different.

- If needed, show the video clip twice to ensure students have adequate time to analyze and determine answers to prompts/questions.

- Suggested uses in English language arts: commercials for elements of persuasion; clips from movies or TV shows for literary elements

- Suggested uses in mathematics: Khan Academy videos to provide students with the "big picture" before the lesson begins; YouTube videos to illustrate real-world applications of the skill to be learned; relevant clips from the TV show *Numbers*

- Suggested uses in science: videos to demonstrate scientific processes and real-world applications; relevant clips from the TV show *House*

(Continued)

(Continued)

- Suggested uses in social studies: clips from historical narratives on the history channel to make the content come to life for the students; television news clips of current events to show real-world connections to content

- Suggested uses in physical education/music/art: videos of professionals demonstrating the skill and/or intended outcome of the lesson

VISUAL REPRESENTATIONS

To activate prior knowledge and get his students thinking critically about yesterday's animal adaptations lesson, Mr. Gerald could have begun Day 2's lesson by showing a visual representation demonstrating the goal he aspired to accomplish. Strategic use of visual representations in the classroom, including photos, symbols, sketches, pictures, and others, helps engage students who have grown up in a media-rich environment where visual representations are readily available. With their heavy use of the Internet, they are accustomed to accessing information in both textual and visual forms. Teaching with visual representations will help develop students' visual literacy skills, which contributes to their overall critical-thinking skills and lifelong learning.

Photos are one type of visual representation that Mr. Gerald could have used to enhance his lesson in a variety of ways. They could engage students in his class who didn't always respond to written materials. Photos would have created a direct, sensory connection between his students and the science lesson that could result in heightened levels of interest and attention. Teaching with photos would also build visual literacy skills in students.

Mr. Gerald's third graders could have analyzed a photo (see page 7) to determine the bird's adaptations and then explained how they are drawing those conclusions (prior knowledge, what has been learned thus far in Mr. Gerald's class, making connections to something in their real world, etc.). This creates an ideal forum for encouraging students to develop their own questions and to learn strategies for answering those questions.

Online resources for finding visual representations:

- http://www.digitalhistory.uh.edu/references/images.cfm
- http://memory.loc.gov/ammem/index.html
- http://guides.library.jhu.edu/images

- http://www.cer.jhu.edu/mediaresources.html
- http://www.ams.org/mathimagery/
- http://www.sciencephoto.com

Visual Representations

Preparation: Choosing and viewing the visual representation ahead of time is critical to ensure it correlates concisely with the standards, goals, and objectives for the topic being studied. A meaningful question/prompt should be developed ahead of time, as well, so students have something meaningful to attend to as they analyze and interpret.

Time Needed: 3–4 minutes

Grouping: Individuals, partners, small groups of 3 or 4

Procedures for Students:

1. Analyze the visual representation and determine its connection to today's lesson.

2. Write (draw, discuss) three observations you can make based on what you are viewing.

3. When time is called, participate in a Stand Up, Hand Up, Pair Up (see Chapter 5) to discuss your findings with others.

4. Be seated after sharing with three partners.

(Continued)

(Continued)

Suggested Adaptations and Applications to Other Content Areas:

- For younger students, ask them to draw or discuss orally with others.
- Give different visual representations to each small group of 3 or 4 instead of one for the entire class.
- Suggested uses in English language arts: pictures of different genres; pictures or symbols representing the conflict or main idea of text to be read
- Suggested uses in mathematics: photos illustrating real-world applications of mathematical skills and concepts to be taught (e.g., aerial photo of a fence surrounding a ranch for area and perimeter)
- Suggested uses in science: photos of real-world events that connect to the content being taught (e.g., picture of an oil spill, photo of a melting glacier)
- Suggested uses in social studies: photos from time period or location being studied; photos from Library of Congress website (www.loc .gov); photos of the same person or event from different perspectives
- Suggested uses in physical education/art/music: a work of art that illustrates the element being studied; a measure of music containing the concept to be taught; picture or diagram of a muscle group that will be used during the lesson

COMICS AND CARTOONS

Another option for Mr. Gerald to kick off this lesson is to use a comic or cartoon to get students thinking critically about animal adaptations.

Comics and cartoons create effective anticipatory sets for two reasons. First, they are typically either humorous or thought-provoking, both of which evoke emotion, causing the brain to produce endorphins. Second, because they must be interpreted, they require critical thinking to unlock their meaning.

Comics and cartoons are quick and appealing because they include more visual input and less text. They provide picture support for reluctant readers and English language learners, giving all students access to the thinking.

Mr. Gerald has found a cartoon centered on how animals adapt for survival (see page 9). He projected the cartoon using the document camera and asked students to write a brief response to the following question: "Based on this cartoon, what do you think we will be learning about today?" He asked students to Stand Up, Hand Up, Pair Up (see Chapter 5) and compare their responses. He then listened in and used their conversations to generate the learning objective for the lesson.

"SINCE WE CAN'T BEAT GLOBAL WARMING, I DECIDED TO TRY TO ADAPT."

Another way that Mr. Gerald could open his lesson using comics and cartoons is to find three cartoons about adaptations, and then make enough copies so that each student can have their own copy of one of the cartoons. Each student would then find three or four other students who have the same cartoon and discuss what the cartoonist was trying to communicate through it. Next, students form groups of three with others who have a different cartoon. They explain their cartoons to each other and look for similarities and differences. Within a few minutes, all the students in Mr. Gerald's class would be discussing animal adaptations and their minds are buzzing with ideas and questions. This would mentally prime them for Mr. Gerald's lesson.

Comics and Cartoons

Preparation: Find three comics or cartoons about the topic of study and print enough copies so that each student has their own copy of one of the cartoons.

Time Needed: 10 minutes

Grouping: Groups of 3

(Continued)

(Continued)

Procedures for Students:

1. Think about the cartoon that was given to you by your teacher.

2. Form a group of three or four with people who are holding the same cartoon.

3. With your group, discuss what your cartoon means and what message the cartoonist is trying to convey.

4. Form a group of three with two other people who are each holding a different cartoon than you.

5. Take turns explaining to each other what your cartoon means and the message the cartoonist is trying to convey.

6. As a group, discuss the similarities and differences in the three cartoons and create a Statement of Insight (see Chapter 6) about what they are communicating.

Suggested Adaptations and Applications to Other Content Areas:

- To make forming groups easier, matte each of the three cartoons on a different color construction paper so that students can group themselves easily by color.

- To reduce the amount of movement, distribute the same cartoon to students who are already sitting together.

- Suggested use for any content area: conduct an Internet search using the search term "Comics AND _____" or "Cartoons AND _____" (insert the specific concept being taught) to find relevant comics and cartoons.

SONGS

Another way Mr. Gerald could have grabbed his students' attention and gotten them thinking about the lesson was to open with a song. According to Chris Boyd and Nusa Maal in their book *Soundtracks for Learning: Using Music in the Classroom* (2008), songs provide opportunities to motivate students and get their attention because "students pay more attention to lessons that are connected with something relevant to their lives and music provides an excellent bridge."

When choosing a song, www.feelgoodsongs.info allows you to search for songs based on ideas, activities, messages, themes, and values. A good resource for printable song lyrics is www.metrolyrics.com. YouTube serves as a great source for all kinds of songs, including ones that have been written and performed by teachers and students about specific content. For professionally produced songs that contain content-rich lyrics that include domain-specific academic vocabulary, visit www.teachbysong.com.

Mr. Gerald found a few songs on YouTube written specifically about animal adaptions, but he really wanted to get his students thinking on a different level. He also considered the fact that a more contemporary song that they enjoyed listening to would spark their interest and engage them. Therefore, Mr. Gerald chose to open his class by playing the chorus to *Survivor*, performed by Destiny's Child (Beyoncé, Dent, & Knowles, 2001). He played it twice, asking students to think about what it might have to do with what they were going to be learning about that day. Every student in the class was sitting up, straining to make out the words to the song. Mr. Gerald directed them to discuss with a partner what they thought they would be learning that day. Some students started out very generally, talking about survival, but as the discussion moved from pairs to whole group, students began connecting yesterday's lesson on animal adaptations to how these adaptations equip animals for survival. Mr. Gerald then asked each pair to create one or two questions about this topic, leading him smoothly and seamlessly into the day's lesson.

Songs

Preparation: Find a song that connects in some way to the content, topic, or concept being taught.

Time Needed: 5 minutes

Grouping: Pairs

Procedures for Students:

1. Listen to the lyrics of the song being played.

2. Based on the words of the song, predict what you might be learning today.

3. When directed, discuss your predictions with a partner, justifying them with the song's lyrics.

4. Be prepared to share a summary of your predictions with the class.

5. With your partner, write one or two questions you have about today's topic.

(Continued)

(Continued)

Suggested Adaptations and Applications to Other Content Areas:

- Print the lyrics to the song to support the verbal linguistic learners.
- For younger students, show animated music videos with lyrics on the screen to provide more purposeful engagement.
- Suggested uses for all content areas: search YouTube for content-specific songs written by teachers; www.flocabulary.com provides songs connected to content with the integration of academic vocabulary

COMPELLING QUESTIONS OR QUOTES

Have you ever forgotten something and spent hours trying to remember it? It drives you crazy until you no longer just want the answer; you have to have it. That's what a great opening question or quote does for students.

Lessons, units, and topics are more motivating and energizing when they begin with a question to which students want to find the answer, or an intriguing quote that stimulates curiosity. Not only do these two ideas generate interest and curiosity, they also answer the questions that so many students wonder about: "Why do I have to learn this?" or "Why is this important to know?"

Great questions and quotes also increase cognitive organization of the content by framing it into a meaningful context for personalized understanding. Research shows that when strategic framing of the lesson is done in the first five minutes of a lesson using strategies like questions and quotes, thinking for the rest of the lesson is enhanced because this is when students decide whether they are going to attend to the task or "check out."

LaTasha would have been engrossed in Day 2's lesson had Mr. Gerald begun the lesson with a compelling question or intriguing quote. For example, suppose Mr. Gerald had begun the science lesson with one of the following on the board:

1) *"It is not the strongest or the most intelligent who will survive but those who can best manage change." –Leon C. Megginson*

or

2) *Would it be better for an animal to lose its sight or lose a limb? Why?*

As LaTasha skipped her way into Mr. Gerald's class and read either one, she would have immediately begun to think more deeply about animal survival, mentally comparing and contrasting. This five-minute warm-up would quickly turn into an interactive, purposeful, and engaging lesson that makes everyone—from Mr. Gerald to LaTasha and her classmates—excited and focused.

Compelling Questions or Quotes

Preparation: Choosing the question or quote ahead of time is critical to ensure it correlates concisely with the standards, goals, and objectives for the topic being studied.

Time Needed: 5–7 minutes

Grouping: Individuals, partners, and small groups of 3 or 4

Procedures for Students:

1. Read the question/quote.

2. Respond by completing the learning task associated with the quote. *(The question is already a learning task because students need to answer it.)*

3. Be prepared to share your thinking when time is called.

Suggested Adaptations and Applications to Other Content Areas:

- Very young students can participate in discussion pairs to successfully complete the learning task (either answering the question or responding, using sentence frames, to the meaning of the quote).

- Older students can find quotes or write questions for homework and share for the beginning warm-up/bell ringer activities.

- Suggested use for any content area: conduct an Internet search using the search term "Quotes on _____" (insert the specific concept being taught) to find relevant quotes; use the questions stems from Chapter 2 to create thought-provoking, open-ended questions.

HUMAN CONTINUUM

Mr. Gerald didn't have to show another video clip to engage the students in the continuation of their study on animal adaptations. He could start this lesson by creating a human continuum. In a human continuum, students physically represent how strongly they feel or how much they know about a topic by where they stand on an invisible line. Mr. Gerald could ask students to think about how much they know about how animals use their adaptations to survive. Students who feel they don't have a deep understanding or still have a lot to learn would stand nearer to one end of the line, while those who felt they knew a lot about animal adaptations would stand nearer the other end. Some students would place themselves somewhere in between. Once everyone has a place on the line, Mr. Gerald will "fold" the line in half by asking the students at one end to wrap around, facing the students at the opposite end. Every student will have a partner who is facing him

Classroom Close-Up:
Human Continuum

Before I began my first lesson on the geography of the Middle East, I wanted to activate my students' prior knowledge, so I used a human continuum. I explained to the students that they would form a line based on their familiarity with the Middle East. I told them to line up left to right in a single line from "I know nothing about the Middle East" to "I am an expert on the Middle East" or somewhere in between. Of course, most of the students placed themselves on the "I know nothing" end. However, I then asked them to fold the line in half, so that the "I know nothings" were standing across from the "experts" on the other end and those in the middle of the line were paired together. I then took a pair from each end of the line to form a group of four made up of all levels of familiarity with the Middle East. Each group began discussing what they already knew about the Middle East and what they wondered about it. As I walked around listening in to their conversations, I realized that many of them were surprised at what they actually did know about the Middle East. These conversations provided a great tool to validate what they already knew and to clarify some misconceptions they had about the region. When they wrapped up their small group discussions, every student in the room was ready to find out more about this topic.

—Denesya Kelsey, seventh-grade social studies teacher, Atlanta, GA

or her. Now, at one end of the line students who have a deep understanding are paired with the students who have limited understanding. At the other end of the line the students who placed themselves in the middle are paired together. Mr. Gerald will now take pairs from each end of the line to form groups of four. These groups are comprised of students who have all levels of understanding. The groups will discuss what they know about animal adaptations and what they still wonder about them. Within just a few minutes, every student is focused on the topic and is mentally prepared to dive into new learning.

WHAT'S THE CONNECTION?

What's the Connection? is an anticipatory set strategy that asks students to analyze a set of objects, pictures, or words to determine their connection. Once students have determined the connection, they can begin to make predictions about the content that will be learned.

When students are analyzing anything and looking for connections between them, they are involved in critical thinking, which deeply engages them in the lesson.

Mr. Gerald could have displayed pictures of a porcupine, a bee, and a jellyfish and asked students to discuss what the connection was between the animals. In small groups students begin discussing that all three are animals. Mr. Gerald would push their

Human Continuum

Preparation: No advanced preparation is required.

Time Needed: 8–10 minutes

Grouping: Groups of 4

Procedures for Students:

1. Think about how much you know about the topic.

2. When directed, put yourself on the "invisible line" based on how much you know about the topic.

3. When directed, the person at one end of the line will "wrap" the line, so that each person is standing directly in front of the person on the opposite end of the line, forming pairs.

4. Form groups of four by combining pairs from each end of the continuum.

5. With your group of four, discuss what you already know about the topic and what you wonder about the topic.

6. Generate a list and be prepared to share it with the whole group.

Suggested Adaptations and Applications to Other Content Areas:

No adaptations are needed; this strategy is naturally differentiated to meet the needs of all learners and can be applied to any content being taught.

thinking further by asking what another connection would be. He would continue this process until students made the connection that all the animals have adaptations to protect them by causing pain to their predators.

By the time Mr. Gerald introduces the lesson's essential question—"What adaptations do animals use to protect themselves?"—LaTasha is eager to experience the lesson.

What's the Connection?

Preparation: Select and gather the objects, pictures, or words that students will analyze.

Time Needed: 5–7 minutes

Grouping: Individuals, partners, small groups

(Continued)

(Continued)

Procedures for Students:

1. Analyze the objects, pictures, or words to determine how they connected.

2. Make a list of these connections.

3. Based on your findings, predict what will be learned today.

Suggested Adaptations and Applications to Other Content Areas:

- Very young students may be overwhelmed with multiple items so limit the number being compared to two.

- To extend the learning, give different items to different groups.

- Suggested uses in English language arts: give students three books that all address the skill or concept you are teaching (e.g., Shakespeare's tragedies, genres, books with a tragic hero); provide three pictures of actions taking place to introduce verbs

- Suggested uses in mathematics: three objects that have the same geometric shape; three things that are measured in fractions (measuring cups, shoes, ruler)

- Suggested uses in science: three items that represent the same element on the periodic table; three scientific terms

- Suggested use in social studies: three items representing the same geographic area (photo, map, artifact); photos of three events from the same time period; three items or pictures that represent a key vocabulary term

- Suggested uses in physical education/art/music: three pieces of music or works of art that have the same theme or element that is to be taught; three pieces of sports equipment that all require use of the same muscle group

STORYTELLING

To capture his students' attention and draw them into the lesson, Mr. Gerald could have opened with a story.

Since the beginning of time, storytelling has served as a way to communicate information, pass on history, and answer compelling questions. While informational text provides the facts and details and speaks to the mind, a story provides a narrative that speaks to the heart. By making students laugh, cry, or think critically, storytelling activates students' emotions, making learning memorable and meaningful and causing those facts and details to "stick."

Many stories can also serve as metaphors, asking students to compare what they are learning and know little about to something familiar. According to *Classroom Instruction That Works* (Dean, Hubbell, Pitler, & Stone, 2012), metaphors prompt students to identify similarities and differences, which has the greatest potential for increasing student achievement.

Mr. Gerald began his lesson by telling his students an adaptation of *The Animal School*, a fable by George Reavis (1999), in which all the animals try to do the same things. For example, the duck excels in swimming but fails when it comes to running. When he finishes the story, Mr. Gerald asks the students to think about what they see as the problem and the solution to this story. He asks them to stand and circle up with the people sitting at their tables and take turns discussing the problem and solutions and to sit down when they are finished. When everyone is seated, he draws the class back together to share what they discussed. What follows turns into a meaningful discussion about the purpose of the adaptations different animals have and how they are uniquely suited for their survival. Mr. Gerald is able to seamlessly transition from this discussion into that day's lesson, with every student cued in to the learning.

Storytelling

Preparation: Find or create a story that provides a narrative account or creates a metaphor for what is being taught.

Time Needed: 8–12 minutes

Grouping: Groups of 4

Procedures for Students:

1. Listen to the story your teacher tells.

2. When directed, stand and cluster in with the people sitting at your table.

3. Take turns discussing what you learned from the story your teacher told and/or responding to the prompt you were given.

4. Sit down once everyone in your group has shared.

5. Share a summary of your group's discussion with the class.

6. Make connections between the story and the lesson.

(Continued)

(Continued)

Suggested Adaptations and Applications to Other Content Areas:

- The teacher will adapt the complexity of the story based on the students.

- Suggested uses for English language arts: Tell a story about your day using elements of whatever genre you are teaching (e.g., "Once upon a time I went to the grocery store . . .)

- Suggested uses for mathematics: Tell a story about someone who solved a problem using mathematical practices (e.g., "I wanted to get an estimate on carpet for my house, and the carpet company asked me for the measurements. I gave the measurements to them and they gave me a very reasonable estimate. However, when they carpeted my house, it was several times the price they quoted! What happened?" Students will discuss that you measured for area inaccurately and that you probably measured the perimeter instead.)

- Suggested uses for science: Tell a story from the point of view of whatever topic you are studying (a molecule, a cell, an animal, a chemical compound)

- Suggested uses for social studies: Tell a story comparing the concept you are studying with something in everyday life (e.g., "My skateboard wheel broke off and I wanted it fixed, so I took it to an appliance repair shop and told them to fix it. They added a handle to the back and charged me $50! What did I do wrong?" Students will talk about how you should have taken it to someone qualified to fix it and then been specific about what you wanted done. Compare this to participating in government.)

- Suggested uses for physical education/music/art: Share inspirational stories of athletes, musicians, and artists who overcame challenges and succeeded through effort and perseverance

Questions for Reflection

1. How has your thinking changed about using anticipatory sets?
2. Think about a lesson you taught recently or plan to teach soon. Reflect on the following:

   - What strategy for anticipatory sets could you use to "hook your students in" to the content?

   - How might using this strategy change the outcomes or the energy of the lesson?

3. What goal can you set for yourself now that you understand the purpose and implementation of anticipatory sets?

2 Keep Calm and Question On

Creating Quality Questions for Critical Thinking

VIGNETTES

A Teacher's Perspective

Rashid Arnel was excited to ask his next question because he knew his fourth graders had really gotten into the passage they read in their basal readers. "What powered these robots we read about?" he asked his students expectantly. Five hands shot into the air—the same five hands that always shot into the air! The same five students who had already answered his first dozen questions. Frustrated, Mr. Arnel grabbed his cup of Popsicle sticks and pulled one out. "Joey, what powered these robots?" Joey glanced around the room uncomfortably. "Electricity?" he said uncertainly. "No, it was the sun . . . solar power," Anthony blurted out. "Anthony," Mr. Arnel sighed, "you've already had your turn to answer. Let's give others a chance." Defeated, Mr. Arnel pulled out another Popsicle stick.

A Student's Perspective

Li had been fascinated by the passage they had read about robots. She couldn't wait to tell her mom what she had learned. "What powered these robots we read about?" she heard Mr. Arnel ask. "I know this one," she thought. "What was it? It wasn't batteries." When Li saw Mr. Arnel reach for his cup of Popsicle sticks, her hands began to sweat. Why couldn't she remember what powered the robots? Quickly, she began flipping through the pages. Mr. Arnel called on Joey and her heartbeat slowed. Li began to think about all the things she wondered about robots and what they could do. She didn't want to raise her hand though, because Mr. Arnel might think she wanted to answer the question. She would just ask her dad tonight.

On the other side of the room, Anthony's hand popped into the air when Mr. Arnell asked his question. "He looked right at me!" thought Anthony, who began frantically waving his hand. Mr. Arnell called on Joey, but Joey thought it was electricity. Anthony couldn't hold it in any longer. "No, it was the sun . . . solar power!" he said triumphantly. Instead of smiling proudly, Mr. Arnel looked at him disappointedly and told him he already had his turn. "I thought Mr. Arnel liked me," thought Anthony. "I guess not."

WHAT ARE QUALITY QUESTIONS?

Most of us can relate to Mr. Arnel's frustration. Why do the same students always have their hands up when we ask questions? Are we asking the wrong questions? Are we asking the right questions in the wrong way? What does a quality question really look like?

According to Webster's dictionary, quality means to have "a high level of value or excellence." In order for a question to have value, it requires deep thinking and a well-thought response. Consider Mr. Arnel's question about what powered the robots. It can be answered in one word and elicits no discussion or deeper thinking. By using a question taxonomy such as Bloom's taxonomy, he could take that knowledge-level question and transform it into one that requires students to think more deeply and has more than one possible response. For example, by asking students to analyze the possible reasons for using solar power for the robots instead of just identifying the source of power, students must go deeper with their thinking and a variety of responses can be considered and debated.

Quality questions require quality think time. When Mr. Arnell asked his question, five hands shot into the air. His five fastest processors just needed to grab that fact from their memories and spit it out. While they were frantically waving their hands in the air, Li was still processing the question. If students had been asked to consider various reasons the robots were powered by solar energy, in order to frame thoughtful responses, they need time to go back into the text, to compare and contrast the advantages of solar power compared to other forms of energy, to evaluate which of their reasons is the strongest.

Quality questions are Google-proof. Our students ask Siri dozens of questions each day and get immediate responses. As teachers, it is easy for us to get frustrated when students want to use Google to answer our questions. However, if our questions can be Googled, why wouldn't they use it? Instead of criticizing their method, we need to analyze the depth of our questions.

Quality questions should not just be asked by the teacher. Just like Li, the students in our classroom have questions about what they are learning; they just need a structure for posing them. Sometimes we are reticent to ask for questions for fear that the students' questions will "lead us down a rabbit trail." By giving students a structure to create questions and then evaluate their quality and relevance before asking them, we begin to transfer the cognitive load from the teacher to the students and the lesson becomes more student-led.

This chapter includes eight strategies for creating quality questions, providing a structure for all students to think about the questions and respond to them, and opportunities for students to generate quality questions of their own.

WHY IT WORKS

For centuries, teachers have used questions as a teaching tool to assess and activate prior knowledge of concepts and skills. They ask questions to help students uncover what has been learned, to comprehensively explore the subject matter, and to generate discussion and peer-to-peer interaction. Well-designed questions lead to new insights, generate discussion, and promote deeper exploration of subject matter. Too often, however, basic recall and comprehension-infused questions are the typical forms being utilized in classrooms rather than asking higher-level, open-ended questions that promote deeper thinking and require students to analyze, synthesize, and evaluate concepts and ideas.

According to research done by Chin (2007), strategic and intentional teacher questioning has been identified as an essential and crucial element in facilitating effective academic conversations, especially in the area of supporting cognitive engagement because students are challenged with the task of providing justification for their responses, they feel more empowered, and develop more ownership in their own learning.

Do you remember when you were young and all you did was "bug" Mom and Dad with questions—"What is that? Why is the sun bright? How do you cut paper? Who is the president? When will it stop raining?" Human beings are naturally wired to ask questions, and it is an essential component of the process of learning. Yet, as we get older and start school, there is a shift. It's no longer about finding answers to questions but more about responding to teacher-created questions. Student-initiated questions increase higher-order learning by requiring them to analyze information, connect seemingly disparate concepts, and articulate their thoughts.

Therefore, teachers have to walk a fine line between enabling students to be dependent upon them by simply answering questions and asking students to develop their own questions. There must be a time and place for students to take on that responsibility and develop their own abilities to craft questions relevant to them just as Li had done but was afraid to ask in class. Giving students purposeful and meaningful opportunities to practice asking their own questions helps them way beyond the classroom; it prepares them for college and career.

I think Clay Parker, CEO of the Chemical Management Division of BOC Edwards, states it best. When asked what qualities he most wants in a potential employee, he responded:

> "First and foremost, I look for someone who asks good questions," Parker responded. "Our business is changing, and so the skills our engineers need change rapidly, as well. We can teach them the technical stuff. But for employees to solve problems or to learn new things, they have to know what questions to ask. And we can't teach how to ask good questions—how to think. The ability to ask the right questions is the single most important skill." (Wagner, 2008)

STRATEGIES FOR QUALITY QUESTIONING

QUESTION STEMS

Quality questions do not just require time to respond thoughtfully, they also require time to create. The reason that the majority of the 300–400 questions that teachers ask each day (Vogler, 2008) are at the lower end of Bloom's taxonomy, is that those questions are easier to ask and easier to answer. Developing questions that require students to think critically requires careful planning. Question stems are an effective tool for building these kinds of rich questions.

Question Stems Based on Bloom's Taxonomy

Knowledge: These questions ask students to recall or regurgitate facts without understanding.

Can you list three . . .?

Can you recall . . .?

Can you select . . .?

How did _____ happen?

What is . . .?

When did . . .?

When did _____ happen?

Where is . . .?

Which one . . .?

Who was . . .?

Who were the main . . .?

Why did . . .?

Example in English language arts:

Teacher Question: Who were the main characters in the story?

Student Response: The king, the queen, and the princess

Example in mathematics:

Teacher Question: Can you list the factors of 21?

Student Response: 1, 3, 7, 21

Example in science:

Teacher Question: What is a life cycle?

Student Response: The changes in the life of a plant or animal.

Example in social studies:

Teacher Question: When did the Civil War begin?

Student Response: April 12, 1861

Example in physical education/art/music:

Teacher Question: What is a line?

Student Response: A mark between two points.

Comprehension: These questions ask students to demonstrate basic understanding of facts and details.

Can you explain what is happening . . . what

is meant . . .?

How would you classify the type of . . .?

How would you rephrase the meaning . . .?

How would you summarize . . .?

What can you say about . . .?

What facts or ideas show . . .?

What is the main idea of . . .?

Which is the best answer . . .?

Which statements support . . .?

Will you state or interpret in your own

words . . .?

Example in English language arts:

Teacher Question: What is the main idea of this paragraph?

Student Response: The king wants the princess to stay in the tower so she will be safe.

Example in mathematics:

Teacher Question: Can you explain how to determine the factors of 21?

Student Response: Find all the numbers that can be multiplied together to make 21. Those numbers are the factors.

Example in science:

Teacher Question: How would you summarize what we learned about life cycles?

Student Response: Every living thing has a life cycle and that cycle repeats.

Example in social studies:

Teacher Question: Can you explain why the Civil War began?

Student Response: The southern states wanted to secede from the Union, but the northern states wanted to remain one nation.

Example in physical education / art / music:

Teacher Question: Can you explain how this work of art demonstrates the use of line?

Student Response: The artist used lines for the buildings in the background and the streets in the forefront of the painting.

Application: These questions ask students to apply knowledge in a different way.

How would you use . . .?

What examples can you find to . . .?

How would you solve _____ using what

you have learned about . . .?

How would you organize _____ to

show . . .?

How would you show your understanding

of . . .?

What approach would you use to . . .?

How would you apply what you learned to

develop . . .?

What other way would you plan to . . .?

What would result if . . .?

Can you make use of the facts to . . .?

What elements would you choose to

change . . .?

What facts would you select to show . . .?

What questions would you ask in an interview

with . . .?

Example in English language arts:

Teacher Question: What questions would you ask in an interview with the king?

Student Response: "Why don't you think you can keep your daughter safe unless she's locked in the tower?"

Example in mathematics:

Teacher Question: What approach would you use to find the factors of 21?

Student Response: I used color tiles to make arrays of 21. Each array is a factor pair.

Example in science:

Teacher Question: How would you organize these pictures to show the life cycle of a frog?

Student Response: I put them in a circle, starting with eggs at the top and put them in order clockwise to show the continuing cycle of life.

Example in social studies:

Teacher Question: What would have happened if Abraham Lincoln had allowed the southern states to secede from the Union?

Student Response: We would have two separate countries instead of one United States of America.

Example in physical education/art/music:

Teacher Question: How would you show your understanding of the use of line using yarn and tag board?

Student Response: I used the yarn to create a horizon and rays of sun extending from the horizon to the end of the tag board.

Analysis: These questions ask students to break information into parts and closely examine each part, making inferences and drawing conclusions based on evidence about the information as a whole.

How is _____ related to . . .?

Why do you think . . .?

What is the underlying theme of . . .?

What were some of the motives behind . . .?

What inference can you make . . .?

What conclusions can you draw . . .?

How would you classify . . .?

How would you categorize . . .?

What evidence can you find . . .?

What is the relationship between . . .?

Can you make a distinction between . . .?

What is the function of . . .?

What ideas justify . . .?

What do you see as other possible outcomes?

If _____ happened, what might the ending have been?

Example in English language arts:

Teacher Question: What is the relationship between the tower and king's perception of the princess?

Student Response: The tower is like a cage, which shows that the king views his daughter as something he needs to control and tame like a wild animal.

Example in mathematics:

Teacher Question: How are the factors related to the product?

Student Response: The factors can be combined to make the product and when the product is divided by any factor, the quotient is another factor.

Example in science:

Teacher Question: Can you make a distinction between a life cycle and a food chain?

Student Response: A life cycle is the stages any plant or animal goes through, but a food chain shows who eats these plants and animals and what they eat.

Example in social studies:

Teacher Question: What ideas justify the South's desire to secede?

Student Response: The tobacco and cotton farmers drove the South's economy and they needed slavery to make their plantations productive and profitable. They believed that northern states were violating the Constitution by not returning their fugitive slaves.

Example in physical education/art/music:

Teacher Question: What is the function of line in this painting?

Student Response: The artist used thick, broken lines to show his anger and disgust at what was happening in society at that time.

Synthesis: These questions ask students to compile information together to make a change in something or create something new.

What changes would you make to solve . . .?

How would you improve . . .?

What would happen if . . .?

Can you elaborate on the reason . . .?

Can you propose an alternative . . .?

How would you adapt _____ to create a

different . . .?

How could you change (modify) the plot

(plan) . . .?

What could be done to minimize

(maximize) . . .?

What way would you design . . .?

Suppose you could _____ what would

you do . . .?

How would you test . . .?

Can you formulate a theory for . . .?

Can you predict the outcome if . . .?

Can you think of a different way for the . . .?

Example in English language arts:

Teacher Question: Can you think of a different way for the king to protect the princess without locking her in the tower?

Student Response: He could have trained her to fight so that she could protect herself.

Example in mathematics:

Teacher Question: How would you adapt the color tile array strategy to find the factors of a three-digit number?

Student Response: Instead of using arrays, I would divide the product by different numbers to find factor pairs.

Example in science:

Teacher Question: Can you elaborate on how the food chain can impact an animal's life cycle?

Student Response: If an animal is a predator and something in its food chain is not available, the animal could die. If an animal is another animal's prey, it is part of that animal's food chain and will die so the other animal can eat and live.

Example in social studies:

Teacher Question: What would have happened if the United States had become two separate countries?

Student Response: We would not be as strong militarily or economically. Each of the two countries would have constantly been in conflict as they tried to expand, so there probably would have been a war at some point anyway.

Example in physical education/art/music:

Teacher Question: How would you adapt the use of line to create a different mood for this painting?

Student Response: I would use softer, flowing, thinner lines that intersect to create a peaceful, harmonious mood.

Evaluation: These questions ask students to present and defend opinions by making judgments about information, the validity of ideas, or quality of work based on a set of criteria.

Explain why you agree or disagree with the actions/outcomes . . .?

What is your opinion of . . .?

How would you prove/disprove . . .?

Can you assess the value/importance of . . .?

Would it be better if . . .?

What would you recommend . . .?

What advice would you give . . .?

How would you rate the . . .?

What would you cite to defend the actions . . .?

How would you evaluate . . .?

How could you determine . . .?

What choice would you have made . . .?

What would you select . . .?

How would you prioritize . . .?

What judgment would you make about . . .?

Based on what you know, how would you

explain . . .?

What information would you use to support

the view . . .?

How would you justify . . .?

Do you think _____ is a good or bad thing?

How effective are . . .?

Example in English language arts:

Teacher Question: Explain why you agree or disagree with the actions of the king.

Student Response: I agree with his actions because the princess is his only child, and if something happens to her, that family could lose the throne.

Example in mathematics:

Teacher Question: Based on what you know, how would you teach a younger student to find factors of a number?

Student Response: I would use the color array strategy because this gives them a hands-on way to create factor pairs and see them for what they really are.

Example in science:

Teacher Question: What information would you use to support the view that zoos are necessary?

Student Response: The life cycle of an animal can be threatened by many things. In a zoo, the scientists are able to control the outside forces that threaten an animal's survival, which is especially important for endangered species.

Example in social studies:

Teacher Question: What choices would you have made if you were a plantation owner/slave/northern business owner?

Student Response: If I had been a plantation owner, I would have reduced the size of my farm so that I could afford to keep it up with paid labor instead of using slave labor.

Example in physical education/art/music:

Teacher Question: Based on the paintings you have viewed and those you have created, how effective is the use of line in communicating mood and movement?

Student Response: I think line is a very effective way to communicate mood and movement because the weight, curve, and flow of a line can all be manipulated to create and change the mood of a piece.

Mr. Arnel's question "What was used to power the robots?" is at Bloom's level of knowledge. By using the question stem, "What would happen if . . .," he can transform that question into one that requires his students to go to Bloom's level of analysis by asking "What would happen if batteries were used to power the robots instead of solar energy?" Students now have to analyze the text to determine why solar energy was used and compare and contrast solar energy with battery power.

Is there a place for questions at the lower end of Bloom's? Absolutely! Starting with a question that is less cognitively complex can allow the teacher to quickly check for understanding and provide the students with the opportunity to mentally access information they have stored about the topic. This is exactly what happened for Li. Even though she could not answer Mr. Arnel's lower-level question, it sparked questions of her own. Mr. Arnel could ask his students a few higher-level question stems and give

Question Stems

Preparation: Select and prepare question stems for students to use. (This can be on an anchor chart, bookmark, displayed on the board, and so on.)

Time Needed: 8–10 minutes

Grouping: Pairs

Procedures for Students:

- On a piece of scratch paper, write two questions about our topic.
- Use the question stems provided to analyze the level of Bloom's taxonomy.
- If your question is at the knowledge or comprehension level, use a higher-level question stem to reframe your question.
- Trade questions with a partner. Analyze and evaluate their quality by asking each other the following questions:
  - Can you support your determined level of Bloom's taxonomy?
  - Why do you think this question is relevant to the topic?
- Be prepared to ask your question during our academic discussion.

Suggested Adaptations:

- Younger students can be given very simple question stems such as "Why is . . .?" or "Who is . . .?" to create questions.
- This task can be scaffolded for special education or ELL students by doing it as a whole group.
- Students who struggle with this task can be purposefully partnered with a student who can help them frame their thinking.

them the opportunity to create questions. This would not only satisfy Li's curiosity, but it would also promote rigorous thinking about the content.

TEXT-BASED QUESTIONS

Text-dependent questions require students to return to the text to support their answers. This rereading fosters deep thinking, which is the fundamental goal of text-dependent questions. As Mr. Arnel asked his students the question, "What powered these robots we read about?" he experienced several problems that could have been eliminated had a text-based question been given. First, only five students, the same five students, raised their hands to respond to the question. Second, when Joey was chosen, he did so by responding in question format—"Electricity?"—signifying his trepidation in answering incorrectly. Third, Mr. Arnel's question didn't ask students to return to the text to support their answers, which would have built confidence in their abilities to be successful, as was the case with Li. Without structures and strategies in place to push students into the text to search for answers, students are left to their own prior knowledge when answering questions. This is why most of Mr. Arnel's students never raised their hands, answered in question format, and felt anxious.

Text-based questions can only be answered with evidence from the text and focus on academic vocabulary to ideas and themes. The most complex and challenging sections of the text are focused on to help students navigate strategically and prioritize their thinking to enhance reading proficiency.

In order to develop quality text-based questions, perform the following steps:

1. Read the text.

2. Draw a conclusion from the text.

3. Use the text-based question stems to turn the conclusion into a question.

4. Write/type the question and pose to students.

If Mr. Arnel had developed a text-based question to begin his lesson, students would have been more equipped and "comfortable" to respond because they would have had a purposeful opportunity to return to the text to construct a reasonable answer. For example, if he had asked, "Based on the information in the text, why is solar energy the best choice for powering the robots?" students would immediately dive into the text to find evidence that would support their answers. The advantage of asking text-based questions is the motivation and enthusiasm they bring into the classroom because they often times will lead students into new discoveries and insights, confirm what they already know, uncover something important they may have overlooked before, and pique their interest and creativity.

Text-Based Question Stems:

- How does the author let you know that . . .?
- What in the text helps you understand . . .?
- Based on the information in the text, how do you know that/describe . . .?
- What words or phrases in the text explain what _____ means?
- What did the main character do or say that lets you know that . . . .?

Text-Based Questions

Preparation: Read the text for which you are writing the text-based questions ahead of time. Follow the procedure outlined above to ensure accurate questions. Limit the number of questions asked because they take more time, effort, and thinking than the basic comprehension-type questions. Project or write the text-based questions so all students can access equally.

Time Needed: At least 5–6 minutes per question to allow students to think about and frame quality responses

Grouping: Individuals, purposeful partners, triads, quads, or whole group

Procedures for Students:

1. Carefully read the question.

2. Skim and scan the text to find the parts that are relevant in answering the question.

3. Frame the response using one of the following sentence frames:

   a. According to the text _____.
   b. In paragraph _____ the author says _____.
   c. When the text says _____ (insert quote from text) _____ it means _____.

4. Be prepared to share as directed.

Suggested Adaptations:

- Middle and high school students could develop their own text-based questions using the provided steps to guide them and then trade with a peer to answer.

- Younger students could answer text-based questions in guided reading groups (small group instruction) or whole group as the teacher leads.

SIMULTANEOUS RESPONSE TECHNIQUES

When Mr. Arnel asks a question, there are a lot of different reactions in his classroom: Anthony knows the answer immediately and can't wait to share. He is hurt and confused when Mr. Arnel won't call on him and then reprimands him when he correctly answers the question. Li is engaged in the thinking, but she needs more time to think through her response and becomes anxious when she thinks she may be called on and doesn't know the answer. Joey just isn't sure. He hasn't thought a lot about what he read, so he takes a guess at the answer. Mr. Arnel is frustrated. The same five

Classroom Close-Up:
Simultaneous Response Techniques

When I ask a question, I don't want only one student at a time to answer, so I use simultaneous response techniques every time I ask a question. There are probably literally a million ways to implement simultaneous response. Recently, I have gone to using Kahoot. The students love it, and it motivates them through competition. This allows me to see what everyone knows in an instant, and I can immediately adjust my instruction based on this feedback. When I want to take a quick survey of the room for the students' opinion of their own understanding, you can't beat "thumbs up/thumbs down" or "fist to five." Group huddle is my favorite when I want students to deeply discuss a question because it gives everyone the opportunity to respond, and when students sit down, I know they are ready to move the discussion to the whole group.

—Jason Ashley, fourth-grade teacher, Columbia, SC

students always have their hands up, and he really wants to hear from other students in the class, which is why he goes for the Popsicle sticks.

What's the solution? A wise teacher once told me that if a question is good enough to ask, then everyone should have the opportunity to answer it. What this class needed is a simultaneous response technique. A simultaneous response technique provides a structure for all students to think about and respond to a question at the same time.

Technique

1. Teacher poses a question.

2. Think time is provided. *Research by Mary Budd Rowe at Columbia University (1986) found that on average teachers wait only 1 second after asking a question. Adequate think time (at least 3–5 seconds) is crucial to the quality of student responses. It also allows your slower processors to digest the question and formulate a response. It is important to remind students they should not raise their hands during this time while everyone should be thinking.*

3. Teacher implements a simultaneous response technique.

4. Students respond using the technique.

5. Teacher corrects, clarifies, and expands on the response.

Strategies for Simultaneous Response

Knowledge- and Comprehension-Level Questions

- **Whisper to Your Hand:** Students chorally whisper the brief response to their hand, elbow, ceiling.

- **Sit Down/Stand Up:** When answering true/false types of questions, students stand when the answer is true and sit when it is false.
- **Thumbs Up/Thumbs Down:** Same procedure as above.

Application-, Analysis-, Synthesis-, and Evaluation-Level Questions

- **Pair-Shares:** Students take turns sharing their responses with a partner.

    i. **Think-Pair-Share**
   ii. **Write-Pair-Share**
  iii. **Draw-Pair-Share**
   iv. **Stand-Pair-Share**

- **Group Huddle:** Students stand up and form a group of four or five. Take turns sharing your responses with your group. Sit down after all group members have shared.
- **Technology Tools:** Use a program like Kahoot (https://kahoot.it) or Plickers (https://plickers.com) that allows all students to respond simultaneously to a question. After everyone has responded, ask students to analyze the responses and pair-share to discuss why the correct answer is correct, explain why some students chose another answer, and/or how to change an incorrect answer to make it correct. (The timer will need to be adjusted on Kahoot to ensure that students have adequate think time before responding.)

Pair-Shares

Preparation: Prepare question(s) in advance.

Time Needed: 1 minute per question

Grouping: Pairs

Think-Pair-Share Procedures for Students:

1. Think about the question. (Please do not raise your hand during this time.)
2. When directed, take turns sharing your response with a partner, listening reflectively to each other.

Write/Draw-Pair-Share Procedures for Students:

1. Think about the question. (Please do not raise your hand or write during this time.)
2. When directed, write or draw your response.

(Continued)

(Continued)

   3. When directed, take turns reading your response or explaining your drawing to your partner, listening reflectively to each other.

Stand-Pair-Share Procedures for Students:

1. Think about the question. (Please do not raise your hand during this time.)
2. When directed, stand up and turn to your partner.
3. Take turns sharing your responses, listening reflectively to each other.
4. Sit down when both of you have shared.

Group Huddle

Preparation: Prepare question(s) in advance.

Time Needed: 1–3 minutes per question

Grouping: Groups of 4 or 5

Procedures for Students:

1. Think about the question. (Please do not raise your hand or write during this time.)
2. When directed, stand up and face your group.
3. Take turns sharing your responses, listening reflectively to one another.
4. Sit down once everyone has shared.

Suggested Adaptations:

These strategies are naturally differentiated based on the level of questioning and the complexity of the responses.

QUESTIONS OF THE DAY

As teachers, we want our students to know what they are learning and why. This is why we make the learning objectives clear to our students. Often, this is very teacher-driven: we state the learning objective and they listen and many times copy it into a notebook or learning log. In order to transfer more of this responsibility to our students, we can have them create Questions of the Day.

Mr. Arnel wants his students to understand the evolution of robotic technology. He has posted his objective: Today you will learn how robots have changed over time. After stating this objective, Mr. Arnel could ask his students to think about what questions they have about this topic and to write at least two questions in their notebooks. As his students move through the lesson, they keep their questions in front of them and Mr. Arnel reminds them to check in with their questions to see if they have learned anything that helps answer them. Students can make notes and jot information beneath their questions throughout the lesson. Before the class period ends, Mr. Arnel will ask his students to revisit their questions and the information they have gathered in order to formulate an answer to each question. Students can then discuss their questions and answers with a partner or small group and hand them in as an exit ticket. Any question that could not be answered can be assigned as an opportunity to research for homework.

Questions of the Day

Preparation: Objective, essential question, standard, and/or learning target(s) are posted for students.

Time Needed: 5 minutes at the beginning of lesson; 5 minutes at the end of lesson

Grouping: Individuals, then pairs or small groups

Procedures for Students (Beginning of Lesson):

1. Read the objective on the board and think about what questions you have about what we will be learning.

2. In your notebook, write at least two of these questions.

3. Throughout our lesson, listen for information that answers your questions and make notes under the questions.

Procedures for Students (End of Lesson):

1. Reread your questions and the information you gathered during the lesson.

2. In your notebook, write answers to your questions.

3. Take turns sharing your questions and answers with your partner/ small group and ask if they have any information you can add to your answers.

4. Be prepared to turn in your Questions of the Day as an exit ticket.

(Continued)

(Continued)

Suggested Adaptations:

- For younger students, questions could be created as a group and listed on the board or chart paper. As information is gathered through the lesson, students could direct the teacher to add it to the chart. Answers could be created together.

- For ELL and/or special education students, students could create questions and then their questions are posted on the board. Information is gathered as a class and then students create answers and share and compare with their peers.

QUESTIONS FROM HEADINGS

Mr. Arnel's question didn't elicit many responses, and the responses he did receive were guesses or based on what students remembered from reading the day before. When students engage in answering questions that require little thinking, are vague, are confusing, or are irrelevant to understanding, they mentally "check out." Because Mr. Arnel's class had read an informational text about robots the day before, one strategy he could have used to ensure students stayed "checked in" would be to turn the headings found in the text into questions.

We learn something every day by reading. Whether we know it or not, we learn through various reading sources like social media, smartphone applications, history and science books, and newspapers. These texts are informative because they build upon our prior knowledge or feed us with information we did not know. They are written using special text features that allow the reader to easily find key information and understand the main topic. The author will do this by providing text features such as headings, bold/italicized words, photographs and captions, as well as other features that support reader understanding. In Mr. Arnel's case, the headings of the informational text being read could have been emphasized as a way for students to craft meaningful questions that would help them focus on finding key details to support the main ideas from those headings.

Writers use headings for a variety of reasons: to help readers figure out what to expect in an upcoming section, to hint at a main idea, or to organize the text's idea. Turning headings into questions will help students frame their thinking more efficiently to ensure they can identify the main idea or skim and scan to determine which section they need/want to read first. Understanding headings can help students become strategic content-area readers, which is critical to being a college- and career-ready individual.

In Mr. Arnel's class, he could have begun the lesson with a strategy called "Questions From Headings." Students get with a partner and access the text being read together. They find the headings of each section, read each one, and turn into a question that can be answered by reading that section. For example, if one of the headings from the robots text was "Robots Are the Future," then the question could be "How will robots be our future?" or "Why are robots going to be our future?" Then students read that section to find the answer. When all questions have been answered, students now have "the gist" of the text because they have strategically identified the key details from each section in order to build comprehension skills. Students self-assess the quality of their questions by if the question was or was not answered precisely.

Questions From Headings

Preparation: This strategy is completely student-driven. The only preparation involved would be for you to have modeled and practiced how to turn headings into questions and have provided a rationale for doing so ahead of time.

Time Needed: 35–45 minutes (depending upon the number of headings and length of text)

Grouping: Individuals, pairs

Procedures for Students:

1. Skim and scan the text to find the headings.

2. Turn each heading into a question.

3. Write the question either on a sticky note or on the text (if it's yours).

4. Read to find out the answer to each question.

5. Highlight or tag any information in the section that answers your question.

6. Write the answer to your question on the sticky note or sheet of paper.

7. Be prepared to share when time is called.

Suggested Adaptations:

- Younger students could complete this task in guided reading groups with teacher support.

- Special education students (depending on disability) could turn headings into questions orally with no writing.

- An anchor chart could be created with student input of question stems to assist in turning headings into questions and posted for use.

SNOWBALL

Mr. Arnel was frustrated. He was disappointed. And most importantly, he didn't know what to do. When he began his lesson with a question that he thought everyone would be excited to answer, he never imagined that the same five students would respond while everyone else in the class decided to "take a break" from learning. In his mind, he thought students would answer an "easy" question enthusiastically and then he could jump into today's lesson with more excitement and anticipation. As we know, unfortunately, it didn't play out that way for Mr. Arnel.

Mr. Arnel's class needed a strategy that would keep all of them engaged, focused, and excited about learning. Snowball is a strategy that elicits these emotional states in students. There are varied purposes for Snowball, ranging from making predictions, summarizing, justifying thinking, generating questions and answers, and thinking critically. Most important, however, is this strategy is active. Any task that can be provided to students that is active creates deeper learning, higher achievement, better recall, higher-level thinking skills, and is more enjoyed by students. If they feel good about the task, they are more apt to persevere and give more effort to its completion.

Based on what students read yesterday, Mr. Arnel could have started his lesson using the Snowball strategy. Each student would write a question on a sheet of notebook paper (no names on paper). Then they would walk to a designated area in the classroom, stand in a circle, and throw their "snowballs" into a basket; fun in itself. Students would then go to the basket, choose a snowball and return to their seats. They open it up, read the question, answer it (if they can back up their answers with evidence from notes, text, etc.), and generate a new question about the content. They return to the designated area and repeat until time has been called or students become unfocused and disengaged. If the questions cannot be answered, then they become investigations for future lessons, research, or homework assignments.

The Snowball strategy enforces writing, responding to text, critical thinking, justifying, and question generation. The anonymity of the activity encourages students to respond even if they are unsure of the "right" answer.

Snowball

Preparation: No preparation is needed; however, modeling and practice sessions are important to do beforehand to ensure productivity. Make sure students have access to notebook paper and pencils.

Time Needed: 10–15 minutes

Grouping: Individuals

Procedures for Students:

1. Think about a question you have about the content or the text we are reading.

2. Write this question on a sheet of notebook paper.

3. Walk to the designated area when time is called.

4. Crumple your paper into a "snowball" and throw in the basket.

5. Walk to the basket and get a snowball out.

6. Go back to your seat, open up your snowball, and read the question.

7. Craft an answer to the question by using notes, text, and other sources of information as evidence supporting your answer.

8. Write another question on your paper and repeat Steps 3–7.

9. Repeat this process until time is called.

Suggestions for Adaptations:

- This strategy can be used with any content—career education, media, art, music, physical education, and so on. Students craft questions and answers based on what they are learning in those classes.

- Younger students could work with partners to write questions and answers (lots of modeling and practice sessions).

QUESTION GALLERY

Because Mr. Arnel's question allowed for one student to respond at a time and it was the same five students, it was difficult for him to get an idea of who understood the information in the text and who didn't understand. He resorted to using Popsicle sticks to call on students, but Li became too anxious and scared and couldn't have answered his question even if she had wanted to answer. Joey wasn't a quick processor so he was guessing at the answer, and Anthony wanted to be called on to answer but his stick wasn't chosen so he impulsively yelled it. What Mr. Arnel needed was a strategy that would not only focus attention but also give him an opportunity to informally assess his students' understanding. The Question Gallery strategy would have done that.

Question Gallery can be used at any point during a lesson. It can be used at the beginning of a lesson to activate prior knowledge, clear up misconceptions, or review the previous day's learning. It can be used during the lesson as guided practice so students apply understanding to complete a specific learning task related to the content being learned. It can be used at the end of a lesson as a part of reflection and closure to process what was learned and understood during that day's lesson.

Mr. Arnel could have used Question Gallery at the beginning of his lesson to review the previous day's learning about robots. For example, he would write a purposeful question (aligned to objectives and standards) on each piece of chart paper (enough charts to ensure there are only four students at each) and place strategically around the classroom.

Then he would give students time to think about each of those questions by accessing notes, texts, and any other resources already introduced and being used in class. Once enough think time has been given, he would ask each group of four to walk to the area where the charts are located. Once there, students determine who will fulfill the roles of writer (writes the response to the question), the researcher (researches to find evidence for answers from the provided sources of information), the response creator (creates the final answer/response to the given question), and the assessor (assesses the final answer/response to ensure it makes sense, is clearly stated, and fully answers the question). When the signal is given to move, students rotate to the next chart and switch roles. This ensures they experience each role through all of the rotations. The complexity of Question Gallery increases each rotation because students must build upon the previous group's answer/response. Once all charts have been completed, groups

Classroom Close-Up:
Question Gallery

At the end of a unit, I wanted to provide a review, but I really struggled with how to make it meaningful. Question Gallery was a great tool to set this up. Before beginning the lesson, I wrote the review questions on chart paper and hung them throughout the classroom. I put students in groups of four and gave each group a different colored marker. Students decided who would be the writer, the researcher, the response creator, and the assessor for the first round. (I always post a description of each role for students to refer to.) The discussions students have as they research their text and notes and create a consensus answer to the question is priceless! This is meaningful review! After the gallery is complete, students take time to record points they know they need to review, and points they know well. In this sense, it's a great study tool!

—Gina Rodriguez, fifth-grade teacher, Rio Rancho, NM

Question Gallery

Preparation: Chart paper with questions should be posted around the classroom ahead of time. Markers and highlighters should be readily available at each chart paper "station." Sources of information that may be needed beyond student notes and text should be readily available at each station.

Time Needed: 10–12 minutes at each chart to ensure adequate time for complete and thoughtful answers to the questions

Grouping: Groups of 4

Procedures for Students:

Part 1 (show this part of the procedure first)

1. With your group, walk to the area where the assigned chart is located.

2. Determine who will fulfill which role for completion of this task (writer, researcher, response creator, assessor).

3. Use roles to answer the question.

4. Rotate to the next chart when time is called.

5. Switch roles to ensure you will have been in each of the four roles by the end of the rotations.

6. Repeat Steps 3–5 until all questions have been answered.

Part 2 (show this part of the procedure after completion of Part 1)

7. Return to the first chart you worked on with your group.

8. Read all of the answers given and highlight the trends.

9. Use the trends to synthesize into a clear and concise answer.

10. Write the final "A+ answer" on the bottom of the chart paper.

11. Be prepared to share.

Suggested Adaptations:

- To build in more individual accountability, allow each student in the group to individually create their own "A+ answer."

- Younger students could develop answers in small groups with adult support.

return to the first chart they worked on together. They read the answers, highlight the trends they notice in all answers, synthesize those trends into a complete and concise "A+ answer," and write it at the bottom of the chart. Then they read their A+ answer to the other groups when time is called.

INTERACTIVE K-W-L CHART

In order to engage his students in thinking before, during, and after reading the text, Mr. Arnel could have used an interactive K-W-L chart. He would start by introducing the topic and letting his students preview the text. In pairs, they would write on sticky notes things they know (or think they know) about robots and stick them in the K (Know) section of the chart on the board. Next, each pair would write at least two questions they have about robots and stick them in the W (Want to Know) section of the chart. Mr. Arnel would then pull the class together and lead them in organizing the statements in the K column, grouping similar statements together. Next, he would do the same thing in the W column.

Now it is time for students to read the text. As they read, they search for answers to the questions in the W column, and seek to confirm or revise the statements in the K column. As they come across answers to the questions, they write the answer on a sticky note and place it in the L (Learned) column beside the question that it answered. If they read something that confirms a statement in the K column, they can make a checkmark on that sticky note and note the page and paragraph number where they found it. If during their reading they find out that one of the K statements is incorrect or incomplete, they correct or complete the statement and note the page and paragraph where the information was found.

When all students have completed the task, they will observe which questions were not answered in the text and can volunteer to research them independently.

Interactive K-W-L Chart

Preparation: Have pads of sticky notes available (using a different color for each column is helpful); create a K-W-L Chart on the board or on a sheet of chart paper.

Time Needed: 30–45 minutes (depending on the length of the text)

Grouping: Pairs

Procedures for Students:

1. With a partner, preview the text by reading the headings and looking at any pictures, charts, and so on.

2. On sticky notes, write anything you know or think you know about this topic (one fact per sticky note) and place them in the K column of our K-W-L Chart.

3. Next, create at least two questions about the topic and write each one on a different sticky note. Place them in the W column of the K-W-L Chart.

4. Participate with the class as we think about how to best organize the information in the K and W columns.

5. With a partner, read the text for the purpose of answering any of the questions in the W column and to confirm or correct any information in the K column.

6. When you find information that answers a question, write the answer on a sticky note, cite the page and paragraph number, and place it in the L column beside the question it answers.

7. When you find information that confirms a statement in the column, make a checkmark on that sticky note and cite the page and paragraph number.

8. When you find information that corrects or provides more information about a statement in the L column, make the corrections on that sticky note and cite the page and paragraph number.

9. Be prepared to discuss what you learned with a small group.

Suggested Adaptations:

- For younger students, this can be done in small, guided reading groups or whole class.

- To provide more structure and focus, this can be divided into three separate tasks for three defined chunks of time.

- For physical education, art, and music, this can be done using an experience instead of a text. For example, what we know/think we know and want to learn about a sport, a media or artist, or a type of music. After experiencing it, we can add what we learned.

Questions for Reflection

1. How can you use Chapter 2 as a tool for reflecting upon and enhancing your questioning?

2. How has this chapter challenged you to help your students become better questioners?

   • What strategy can you use to facilitate this process?

   • What steps need to be put into place to equip your students to ask deep and meaningful questions?

3. Record yourself for a 30-minute block of time and review the recording.

   • Tally the types of questions you asked.

   • Think about an area of your lesson where you can ask higher-level questions.

   • Use the Question Stems to create more rigorous questions.

3

Let Them Talk

*Structuring Academic Conversations
and Effective Communication*

VIGNETTES

A Teacher's Perspective

Coach Rogers sighs in defeat as he looks at his students silently copying notes from their textbooks. He really wants his lessons to be interactive and engaging for the students. Today, he tried again to get his students to pair-share, but, like always, it turned into one big gossip session. As he walked around the room, all he heard were conversations about tonight's football game and who was dating whom. He put a stop to that really fast by telling them that since they couldn't handle talking about their learning, they could spend their time copying notes from the book. Coach Rogers shook his head in frustration. He didn't want to teach like this, and he knew they didn't want to learn like this, but what else could he do?

A Student's Perspective

Ashley felt confused as she laboriously copied notes from her textbook into her notebook. Coach Rogers was mad at them again, and this was their punishment. What they were being punished for, Ashley wasn't sure. Coach Rogers asked them to share with their partners which event brought the United States into World War II. She turned to Heather and told her it was the bombing of Pearl Harbor and Heather agreed. While everyone was finishing up, Heather told her that Ryan had broken up with Sandy and had asked Lauren out. They weren't talking loudly or interrupting the other groups. So why is Coach Rogers so upset?

WHAT IS ACADEMIC DIALOGUE?

Coach Rogers understands that when students are thinking, talking, and working, that is when they are learning. His problem is one that many of us have experienced. How do we make sure students are talking about the content, and not just talking? Coach Rogers needs to structure an academic dialogue so that students have more to discuss than just a phrase that answers the question.

According to Dr. Cathy O'Connor of Boston University (n.d.), rich, meaningful academic conversations occur when "teachers skillfully encourage their students to think deeply, articulate their reasoning, and listen with a purpose." In order for this to happen, teachers must do four things:

1. Create a structure for both the speaking and listening.
2. Provide sentence stems to frame appropriate academic dialogue.
3. Hold students accountable for information discussed.
4. Require that evidence be used to support discussion.

Often the reason student discussions are not academically productive is because students struggle to get the conversation started and keep it focused on the topic. These conversations can actually detract from the learning, rather than enhancing it. The goal is to create an actual dialogue where students respond to each other and build on the ideas of one another, not just taking turns talking and listening. The following sentence stems help students start the academic conversation appropriately and guide them in responding to each other.

- I believe _____ because _____.
- I agree with _____ because _____.
- I disagree with _____ because _____.
- I'm confused. What did you mean when you said _____?
- On page _____ it says _____ so I think _____.

This chapter contains eight strategies for academic dialogue that incorporate the four components of rich, meaningful academic conversations.

WHY IT WORKS

At the heart of a productive academic conversation is the ability to communicate effectively. Good communication skills are key to, not only school success, but success in life, work, and relationships. Without effective communication, the message can turn into a misunderstanding by being misinterpreted or poorly delivered.

Academic conversations are meaningful communication tools that help *all* students develop critical reasoning skills and deepen understanding of content and multiple perspectives. It is through this conversation that teachers constructively intervene by pushing students to think deeply, organize their thoughts into sentences, negotiate meaning, back claims with evidence, ask for clarification, and construct meaning in real time as the dialogue develops.

Research has shown that proper use of academic conversations can strengthen teacher–student rapport, create an open and supportive learning environment, and provide students with new ways of exploring information that can lead to deeper understanding of new concepts.

Giving students more opportunities to talk and discuss knowledge extends what Cazden (2011) calls "speaking rights," which traditionally have been closely held by teachers. Allowing students to voice their opinions, make personal connections to content, and develop insights about their own learning makes them part of a group that helps to define true understanding. Meaning and language can be developed simultaneously through contextualized problems that require students to talk about what they are learning as they are learning it. At first the language may not be precise, but as students continue to work together and talk with one another and the teacher, the underlying meanings of the words evolve (Kotsopoulos, 2007). As students engage in this discourse they acquire new ways of talking and thinking.

Because it is an intentional and purposeful process, planning for it is critical because its use is different from everyday language. Some students are not exposed to this language outside of school. Much of the academic discourse is discipline-specific and deepens subject matter thinking. Unless we make academic discourse transparent for learning, many students will be excluded from classroom discussion that depend on having acquired this language. By providing a format to make hidden thought processes more public and shared, skilled thinkers and language users are equipped to pass on skills and ideas to others.

STRATEGIES FOR ACADEMIC DIALOGUE

REFLECTIVE DIALOGUE

Coach Rogers did what many frustrated teachers do every day. He didn't know what else to do when the students started having side conversations about unrelated topics so, in order to "focus" them on the appropriate topic, he made them copy notes. He knew it wasn't the most effective way for students to spend their time in his class, but what else could he do when they refused to discuss what he intended for them to discuss?

Effective and purposeful discussions seldom just happen. It takes talent and planning to make them worth the time and energy. As teachers, we play vital roles in guiding the academic nature and depth of a discussion. Reflective Dialogue is a strategy for ensuring these conversations are focused and intentionally aligned to content being learned in class so students have to critically think, extend, revise, and clarify to develop knowledge and understanding. Structuring reflective dialogue in the form of "sentence frames" provides a scaffold for students to proficiently use the challenging and complex academic language in meaningful contexts. One way of designing this is by giving students a meaningful, relevant, open-ended question related to the content that will provide a structure for which they begin digging deeper and asking more questions.

Coach Rogers could have begun his lesson by asking a relevant question to shape the conversation and push his students to think critically and engage with the day's content. If he had asked the following question:

> *"Do you agree or disagree with the United States' entry into World War II? Use evidence from your notes and text to support your viewpoint. Use this sentence frame when discussing with a peer: I agree/disagree with the U.S. entry into WWII because _____. I base my viewpoint on _____ from my notes and _____ from the text."*

Students are then proactively and mentally engaged in rich, reflective conversation and being held accountable for the answer by allowing them to come up with more thoughtful, lengthy, and personalized responses using sentence frames that demonstrate what they have learned about Coach Rogers' content thus far in his unit of study on U.S. history. In this scenario, the design of the question sharpens students' thinking by reinforcing their abilities to build and use knowledge to answer the question and construct meaning as the academic conversation develops.

Reflective Dialogue

Preparation: Clear and concise procedures for collaborative work (partners and small groups) must be introduced, modeled, and practiced ahead of time to ensure productivity. A thoughtful and rigorous question should be developed prior to the lesson so students have something of substance to discuss with partners or small groups. Provide sentence frames, as modeled in the above example, to ensure students have opportunities to articulate their thinking effectively.

Time Needed: 5–7 minutes

Grouping: Partners

Procedures for Students:

1. Read the question.

2. Access your notes and textbook to answer the question.

3. Write/type your answer using the provided sentence frame.

4. Partner with a peer and share your responses.

5. Use the following response frame to assess each other's thinking:

    "I agree/disagree with your viewpoint because _____."

Suggested Adaptations:

- Younger students could practice reflective dialogue during guided reading time to ensure they learn how to do this effectively as they receive support from the teacher.

- Reflective dialogue could be an oral task instead of a writing task.

The more adept students become in using reflective dialogue, the more precise and skilled they will become as critical thinkers and communicators, and having the ability to pass on ideas and skills to others.

SOCRATIC SEMINAR

Coach Rogers has enjoyed facilitating small group discussions in his class, but he really wants to have a whole group discussion on the bombing of Pearl Harbor. He decides to try a Socratic seminar.

His students have read and annotated two articles about the bombing of Pearl Harbor. He pairs his students up, and each pair writes two questions based on the information in the articles. Students then move half of the desks against the walls and arrange the other half into a circle. One person from each pair sits in the desks arranged in a circle, while the others stands behind their partners. Coach Rogers adds an empty desk to the inner circle. Ashley starts the seminar by asking the question she wrote. Chris responds to her question. Gia responds to Chris using one of the response frames that Coach Rogers posted on the board. Coach Rogers makes notes of who has contributed to the seminar. The students in the outer circle make notes about things they have heard that are interesting and/or important. Tara leaves the outside circle and sits in the empty chair in the inner circle. She uses one of the response frames to respond to a comment she just heard. When the discussion shifts to another question, Tara returns to the outer circle. Coach Rogers wants the students to discuss the impact of internment camps, but no one has brought that up, so Coach Rogers sits in the empty chair and asks the inner circle whether internment camps were necessary. As students respond, Coach Rogers vacates the chair and makes eye contact with Damion, cueing him that he hasn't yet contributed to the conversation.

After all students in the inner circle have contributed to the discussion, Coach Rogers asks the outer circle to switch places with the inner circle and the Socratic seminar continues.

Suggested Response Frames

- I agree with _____ (insert student name) because _____.
- I agree with _____ (insert student name), and something I can add is _____.
- I disagree with _____ (insert student name) because _____.
- I have a question about _____ (insert student name)'s comment:

Socratic Seminar

Preparation: Students need to have read and annotated a text and worked with a partner to create two questions to use in the seminar.

Time Needed: 45 minutes

Grouping: Whole class

Procedures for Students (Inner Circle):

1. Anyone may begin our seminar by posing his or her question.

2. Any student may respond to the question.

3. Add value to the conversation by responding to the previous speaker using one of the response frames.

4. When a question has been exhausted, anyone may pose a new question.

5. Seminar continues. (Remember that all students need to actively participate.)

Procedures for Students (Outer Circle):

1. Stand behind your partner and listen reflectively to the seminar.

2. Make notes of any information you hear that you feel is new, important, or insightful.

3. If you have a question or want to respond to something that has been said, join the inner circle by sitting in the empty chair.

4. Return to the outer circle after your point has been addressed.

5. Be prepared to share your recorded insights with the class.

Suggested Adaptations and Applications to Other Content Areas:

- Once students have mastered the process, multiple smaller inner circles can occur simultaneously.

- Seminar can be done with only an inner circle with the teacher a part of the inner circle in order to provide guidance and maintain flow.

- Suggested use in English language arts: discuss a poem, section of a story or article, or similarities and differences between the book and the movie version of a novel

- Suggested use in mathematics: discuss various problem-solving strategies or come to the seminar with questions you have about the content

- Suggested use in science: discuss an article on a current issue in science such as genetic engineering

- Suggested use in social studies: read two different perspectives of the same historical event and discuss

- Suggested use in physical education/art/music: read and discuss articles on famous athletes, composers, musicians, and artists

PLAYING CARD DISCUSSION

Coach Rogers is frustrated when he hears his students talking about things other than history. The problem is that he hasn't structured enough for them to talk about. A playing card discussion would provide this structure.

Coach Rogers could create three or four rich questions about the bombing of Pearl Harbor and post them on the board. Instead of numbering

Classroom Close-Up:
Playing Card Discussion

As a remedial reading teacher, I use a scripted program that includes comprehension questions with each reading selection. I wanted the students to really get into a discussion around the questions, but once one student had answered, the others seemed to think that question was "done" and were ready to move on. I decided to try adding some structure to our discussions using the Playing Card Discussion strategy. I took the three or four richest questions straight from the book and put a playing card suit next to each one. Then I gave a playing card to each student. First, they grouped up by suit and discussed the question that matched that suit. This gave them a chance to collaboratively create a comprehensive response to the question and gather evidence from the text to support the answer. Next, they would meet up with those students having the same number. Since each one had a different suit, they could each lead a discussion about their own question. This allows more students to be involved in the discussion, but also for more discussions to be going on at once.
— Wendy McDaniel,
middle school reading specialist,
Tulsa, OK

the questions, he could put a playing card suit next to each (see Image 3.1). He would give each student a playing card and ask them to think about the question that matches their suit. He might decide he wants them to jot down some information that answers the question and/or go back into the text or their notes and gather evidence to support their responses. Next, the students would form a group with others who are holding the same number card. This creates groups of students who all thought about a different question. Students then take turns sharing their responses, asking if anyone else in the group has anything to add, creating a rich collaborative conversation about the topic.

The Playing Card Discussion strategy can be used with any subject. For example, in math, the teacher could put a different problem next to each suit. When students form groups, they discuss the strategy they used to solve the problem and other students in the group could offer ideas for other strategies that could be used to solve the problem.

Playing Card Discussion Questions

 SPADES: How has your thinking changed after reading this book?

 CLUBS: Discuss the setting of the book. Why is it important to the story? How would the story be different set in another place or time?

 DIAMONDS: Discuss the most important event(s) in the book. Why were they so important to the development of the plot?

 HEARTS: Discuss the theme of the book. What message is the author trying to communicate, and how does he or she do it?

Playing Card Discussion

Preparation: Take out the number of cards to match the number of students, making sure you have 3 or 4 of each number. If the number of students doesn't come out even, use Jokers as wild cards (students can choose any suit and any number). Write three or four questions, problems, or prompts and display with a playing card suit next to each one.

Time Needed: 8–10 minutes

Grouping: Groups of 3 or 4

Procedures for Students:

1. Think about the question that matches the suit of your playing cards and create a response.

2. Form a group with those who are holding the same number playing card.

3. Take turns sharing the response to your questions. Be sure to ask if anyone has anything to add.

4. Listen reflectively to one another.

5. Return to your seats when all questions have been discussed.

Suggested Adaptations and Applications to Other Content Areas:

- To further scaffold the discussion, students can first form a group with others who have the same suit and discuss that one question, ensuring that everyone has a clear, correct response to share with their number group.

- Suggested use in English language arts: each suit discusses one of the following after reading a piece of fictional text: characters, setting, plot, theme

- Suggested use in mathematics: each suit discusses one of the following after solving math problems: challenges/misconceptions, alternate strategies, which problem helped them better understand the overall concept and why, or students can discuss questions interpreting charts and graphs

- Suggested use in science: each suit discusses one of the following after completing a lab: what surprised me, what conclusions I draw, evidence from the text to support what happened

(Continued)

(Continued)

- Suggested use in social studies: each suit discusses one of the following after reading/listening/watching a speech or another primary document: what insights this speech/letter/diary entry gives you about this person, what insights this speech/letter/diary entry gives you about this period in history, what you would have added to this speech/letter/diary entry to make it more powerful or provide additional clarity

- Suggested use in physical education/art/music: questions can be discussed after listening to a piece of music, observing works of art, or watching a video of an athletic event; questions can include analysis of the message being communicated through the work, skills necessary to achieve this level of performance, impact of this work or event on culture

THINK DOTS

Coach Rogers' goal is always to provide interactive and engaging activities in his classroom so students will like being there. He gets irritated and feels defeated each time he tries to do things that will make it fun but nothing seems to work with "these kids" so he always finds himself going back to doing the only thing he knows he can do to make them work: copying notes.

When students arrived to Coach Rogers' class, had he implemented the Think Dots strategy, he would have immediately seen a shift in the level of conversation, a shift in the level of focus and a shift in the level of engagement. Think Dots is an effective strategy for students to construct meaning for themselves about the concept they are studying. It naturally leads students into deeper exploration and elaboration as they participate in small group academic conversations with peers. Coach Rogers would develop six questions (ones that relate

Classroom Close-Up: Think Dots

I use Think Dots all the time to get students to discuss comprehension questions from our reading selections. I put the questions into a Think Dots template and make a copy for each student. I divide students into groups of 4–6 students. One student in each group rolls the die and begins the discussion on the question that matches the number on the die. Once that question has been thoroughly discussed, each student writes a summary response on his or her Think Dots sheet. The die is passed to the next student and play continues. I love listening to students discuss the questions and explain their thinking!

—Faith Kendall, third-grade teacher, Blythewood, SC

THINK DOTS

Do you agree or disagree with the United States' entry into World War II? Use evidence from your notes and text to support your viewpoint.

Compare and contrast George W. Bush's speech to the American people on September 20, 2001, with Roosevelt's "Day of Infamy" speech. Does each speech accomplish its purpose? Is one speech better than the other? Why? Use evidence from the speeches to support your answers.

How do you think young Americans your age reacted to the news of Pearl Harbor? In what ways did the coming of WWII to the United States affect students your age? Cite evidence to support your answer.

Compare and contrast these events.

Everett Historical/Shutterstock.com

Dan Howell/Shutterstock.com

What were some of the outcomes of the Pearl Harbor attack? What role do you think Roosevelt played in leading the nation during this era?

Explain why December 7, 1941, is considered the most important day of Roosevelt's presidency.

Think Dots

Preparation: Choosing rigorous questions, typing the questions into the Think Dots template (see Appendix), one die, and individual copies of the Think Dots sheet should be prepared in advance.

Time Needed: 45–60 minutes (depending on questions and time frames)

Grouping: 2–4 students per group

Procedures for Students:

1. Roll the die.

2. Look for the corresponding die on your Think Dots sheet.

3. Read the question or prompt.

4. Share your answer.

5. Listen reflectively as others synthesize and record your answer on their Think Dots sheet.

6. Give the die to the next person in your group.

7. Repeat steps 1–6 until all questions/prompts have been answered.

Suggested Adaptations and Applications to Other Content Areas:

- Very young students can use Think Dots to practice foundational skills such as letter sounds, counting, rhyming words, long and short vowels, and so on.

- If technology is available, Think Dots can be used through Google Docs or other formats.

- If paper supply is an issue, project the Think Dots onto the screen and students write answers on a sheet of paper equally divided into six parts.

- Suggested use for English language arts: vocabulary, revisions for writing, editing sentences for conventions and mechanics, questions about a story or article (could be the questions in your teacher's manual)

- Suggested use for mathematics: word problems, math problems to demonstrate, mathematical terms, analyzing incorrectly solved problems for errors

- Suggested use for science: science terms, questions at the end of a chapter, questions to reflect on a lab

- Suggestions for social studies: academic vocabulary, finding locations on a map, questions at the end of a chapter

- Suggestions for physical education/art/music: vocabulary, questions to analyze a work of art or piece of music, various athletic skills or exercises for students to perform (e.g., dribbling, passing, sit-ups, burpees)

to goals, objectives, and content standards) and place in a Think Dots template (see Resources). When students arrived, each group would be given Think Dots sheets (one per person), one die, and the procedures would be posted on the board. Students then take turns to answer the questions given based on the number they roll. As one student rolls the die, finds the corresponding number on the Think Dots sheet, and answers the question, the other student synthesizes the answer into his or her own words and writes it in the box. Play continues until all questions have been answered (see page 59).

Since Coach Rogers' goal is to provide interactive and engaging learning tasks for his students to ensure they remain focused on content, Think Dots would be a powerful and student-driven way to make that happen. Students would leave his class feeling accomplished, energized, and looking forward to the next day's lesson.

EQUALIZED DISCUSSION

Coach Rogers really wants productive academic conversations to occur in his classroom, but he has some students who take over and monopolize the conversations while others are so quiet, they hardly say a word. He feels most frustrated with the students who are content just to sit back and let others do the thinking and talking. The Equalized Discussion strategy is just what Coach Rogers needs!

Coach Rogers wants his students to compare and contrast the bombing of Pearl Harbor with the terrorist attack on the World Trade Center on September 11, 2001. He divides his students into groups of four and gives each student four pennies. Students begin to discuss the similarities and differences between Pearl Harbor and 9/11. Each time a student adds unique information to the discussion, he or she slides a penny to the top edge of the desk. Students know that once all their pennies are spent, they can no longer contribute to the conversation, and that each person must spend all his or her pennies. Coach Rogers is thrilled to see one of his English language learners contributing to a discussion for the first time. He is also relieved that he doesn't have to go over to Ashley's group and remind her to let others have their turns to speak.

Equalized Discussion

Preparation: Find 2–6 markers (poker chips, pennies, paperclips, Unifix cubes, etc.) per person (enough markers for each group can be put into resealable bags to streamline this process).

(Continued)

(Continued)

Time Needed: 10–20 minutes (depending how many markers you give each student)

Grouping: 4 students per group

Procedures for Students:

1. Discuss the topic with those at your table.

2. When you contribute new information to the discussion, put a marker at the top of your desk.

3. Remember the following:
   • You cannot use one of your markers for simply agreeing with what another member said; you must add your own information.
   • You must use all of your markers.
   • After you have used all your markers, you may not speak.

4. Listen reflectively to each other and add value to the conversation.

Suggested Adaptations:

   • This can also be done with pairs or groups of three.
   • This strategy is differentiated based on the number of markers students use.

TALKING TRIADS

Ashley was confused by Coach Rogers' attitude toward her and the other students because all of them were doing what he had asked them to do. The problem was that they were finished answering his question and had other things they wanted to talk about so they filled their "lag" time with informal conversation. In Coach Rogers' mind, he wanted them elaborating and discussing in depth beyond what the question was asking. Because this wasn't occurring and because there were only certain students participating anyway, he resorted to copying notes.

   If Coach Rogers' vision was to put students into small groups so they could have meaningful academic conversations, a strategy he may want to try is called Talking Triads. Talking Triads is a group of three students taking an active part in a focused conversation with each student having a different role: (1) speaker—speaks first and discusses the given topic or answers the given question, (2) reflective listener—listens to the speaker and summarizes what was shared, and (3) observer/analyst—observes both the speaker and reflective listener and provides comments and feedback about the discussion, and relates discussion back to learning outcomes, goals, key words, and any other critical elements deemed important by the teacher.

For instance, suppose Coach Rogers posed the following three questions:

1. Do you agree or disagree with the United States' entry into World War II? Use evidence from your notes and text to support your viewpoint.

2. What were some of the outcomes of the Pearl Harbor attack? What role do you think Roosevelt played in leading the nation during this era?

3. Explain why December 7, 1941, is considered the most important day of Roosevelt's presidency.

He then strategically places students into groups of three and provides them with the three questions he wants discussed. He places the procedures on the board, asks students to determine first-round roles (speaker, reflective listener, observer/analyst) and, starting with the first question, asks them to begin the Talking Triads process. As students begin, Coach Rogers will be amazed at the level of engagement and how in-depth students take themselves in deepening their understanding of the social studies content. He will be excited. His students will be focused. And everyone will leave class feeling accomplished and empowered.

Talking Triads

Preparation: Strategically place students into groups of three in advance, have three meaningful questions prepared for the discussion, provide the defined roles, and make sure you have modeled and practiced what it should look and sound like in the Talking Triad groups if students are following expectations.

Time Needed: 15 minutes (5 minutes for each rotation)

Grouping: Groups of 3

Procedures for Students:

1. Get into your assigned talking triad.

2. Determine who will be the speaker, reflective listener, and observer/analyzer for the first round.

(Continued)

(Continued)

3. Participate in your role using the following:

   a. Speaker—you will begin by reading and answering Question 1
   b. Reflective listener—you will reflectively listen to the speaker and summarize what was shared using the sentence frame "What I heard you say was _____."
   c. Observer/analyst—you will observe both the speaker and reflective listener and provide comments and feedback about the discussion and any other critical elements deemed important by the teacher

4. Rotate seats and read the procedures for your new role (a–c) except this time the speaker will begin by reading and answering Question 2.

5. Repeat Step 4 with Question 3.

Suggested Adaptations:

- Prepare a different set of questions or prompts for younger students.

- Art students can bring their products to the talking triads to use as prompts for discussion.

CONTENT COFFEEHOUSE

Coach Rogers has tried some different strategies to structure small group academic conversations. He is pleased with the level of student involvement, but he has found that a few of his students have especially rich points to add to their conversations and wishes more students could hear that level of thinking. Implementing a Content Coffeehouse would make this happen.

After teaching about the bombing of Pearl Harbor, Coach Rogers asked the students to think about what happens at a coffee shop. He guided them to a discussion of the fact that there are a limited number of tables in most of their local coffee shops, and many times a stranger will ask if he or she can share your table. He also brought up that when this happens to him, he and the stranger often strike up a conversation about something they have in common like sports, books, or movies. If his tablemate mentions a book or movie he might be interested in, Coach Rogers jots the title on a napkin. With this discussion, he is setting the stage for a Content Coffeehouse.

Students arrange their desks in groups of four to create a tabletop. Coach Rogers gives each student a paper napkin and instructs them to begin a conversation about the bombing of Pearl Harbor. He reminds them that if they hear something that is new, interesting, or important to them, to jot it down on the napkin. He has set a timer for four minutes. When the timer sounds, he asks students to number off 1–4. He tells the twos and fours to stand up and join a new table, but they can't go to the same table. Once these students are seated, Coach Rogers prompts them to begin the conversations at their new tables by sharing something interesting they heard at their last table, referring to the notes on their napkins. This process continues for one more round. Students then return to their seats and reread the notes they have made on their napkins. They then write a brief summary of what they discussed in their notebooks. Students share these summaries with a partner.

Content Coffeehouse

Preparation: Provide one napkin per student; pencils will not work well for this task, so have some ballpoint pens on hand if students need one. A timer is also needed.

Time Needed: 18–20 minutes

Grouping: Groups of 4

Procedures for Students:

1. Discuss the topic with those at your table.
2. When you hear something new, interesting, or important that you want to capture, jot it down on your napkin.
3. When the timer sounds, number yourselves 1–4.
4. Listen for which students will move.
5. When all students are seated at their new tables, one of the newcomers should begin the conversation by sharing something he or she heard at the last table.
6. Continue the process as directed.
7. When directed, return to your seat and read through the notes on your napkin.
8. Create a brief summary of your learning in your notebook.
9. Be prepared to share your summary with a partner.

Suggested Adaptations:

- Younger students can write a word or draw a picture on individual dry erase boards to capture their learning.
- Notes can be made on cell phones instead of napkins to emulate real-world notetaking.

CLOCK APPOINTMENTS

As Coach Rogers observed students in his class talking with each other off-topic, he became frustrated because all he wanted them to do was have a rich, academic conversation and they couldn't "handle" it. How many times has that happened to you? As teachers, we experience this scenario more times than we would probably like to admit. In Coach Rogers' situation, he could have implemented the strategy called Clock Appointments to help students be more attentive and focused on academic conversations instead of the gossip sessions they were having.

Clock Appointments is a strategy that can be used at the beginning, middle, and end of a class. When used at the beginning of class, students could be answering questions about a new topic so the teacher could assess quickly where to take the lesson next. It could be used during the lesson as a structure for practicing the content introduced at the beginning of class, and it could be used at the end of class as a way to demonstrate understanding of that day's lesson. The goal is to find three people with whom to schedule appointments at the hour, quarter hour, the half hour, and the 45-minute mark. The teacher begins by showing the procedure for Clock Appointments. Students walk around the room and freeze when the music stops playing (refer to Chapter 5, "Mingle to Music"). They partner with the person closest to them and this becomes their first appointment (12:00). They write the person's name down on their clock (see template in Resources) in the 12:00 slot so they remember it throughout the class period or throughout the day. Then they discuss the question that is paired with the time. When the music begins again, they walk and freeze when the music stops. They partner with the person closest to them and this becomes the next appointment (3:00). They write the person's name down on the clock in the 3:00 slot so they remember it throughout the class period or throughout the day. Then they discuss the question that is paired with the time. This process is repeated two more times (6:00 and 9:00) to ensure each student has four different "Clock Appointments" throughout the class period or throughout the day.

Now let's take a look at how Coach Rogers' class discussion could look and sound if he implemented Clock Appointments (see page 67).

Now as Ashley walks around the room and the music stops, she isn't standing close enough for Heather to become her partner. She is close to Chris, however, and he becomes her first appointment (12:00). After Ashley writes Chris' name on the 12:00 line and Chris writes Ashley's name on the 12:00 line, they read the question and take turns discussing their thoughts. When the music begins playing, Ashley and Chris give each other high

Clock Appointments

Do you agree or disagree with the United States' entry into World War II? Use evidence from your notes and text to support your viewpoint.

How do you think young Americans your age reacted to the news of Pearl Harbor? In what ways did the coming of WWII to the United States affect students your age? Cite evidence to support your answer.

What were some of the outcomes of the Pearl Harbor attack? What role do you think Roosevelt played in leading the nation during this era?

Explain why December 7, 1941, is considered the most important day of Roosevelt's presidency.

fives and they move on. This process continues until every student has received four appointments and has discussed the essential questions that Coach Rogers had prepared. Now that his students are equipped to work with three other learning partners, he proceeds into his direct instruction. When direct instruction is complete, he quickly asks students to get with their 9:00 appointments to complete a learning task comparing and contrasting the events of September 11 and the Pearl Harbor attack. It is then that he realizes that the Clock Appointment strategy is not only an effective structure for increasing academic conversation but also a classroom management tool that increases time on task and learning time.

Clock Appointments

Preparation: Create the prompts or questions that should be included on the Clock Appointments sheet (see Resources), make individual copies of the Clock Appointments sheet, and prepare music to play.

Time Needed: 5–10 minutes

Grouping: Partners

Procedures for Students:

1. As the music plays, walk around the room.

2. Freeze when the music stops.

3. Partner with the person closest to you.

4. Write his or her name in the appropriate appointment time.

(Continued)

(Continued)

5. Take turns discussing the question that matches the appointment time.

6. Repeat Steps 1–5 until you have four appointments.

Suggested Adaptations:

- Younger students could find one appointment and that becomes his or her partner for the entire day or week.

- Use the structure for an entire week to quickly partner students.

Questions for Reflection

1. Analyze who is doing most of the talking in your classroom.

    - If it is you, which strategies will you implement to begin to turn this responsibility over to your students?

    - If it is the students, which strategies will you implement to deepen their academic conversations?

2. Observe your students having an academic conversation.

    - What formative assessments were you able to make by listening in on their conversation?

    - What scaffolds or supports are still needed to ensure productive academic conversation?

4 Two Heads Are Better Than One

Strategies for Effective Collaboration

VIGNETTES

A Teacher's Perspective

Keniesha Glover was exhausted and it wasn't even lunch time! Her administrator had gone to yet another conference and was insisting that students collaborate. What Dr. Johnson didn't understand was that these kids didn't know how to work in groups. Take this morning, for instance. Keniesha had divided her fifth graders into groups of four—Dr. Johnson said that was the magic number—and asked them to read the story in their basal together and then answer the questions at the end. As she walked around the room, some students were reading silently, some were reading in pairs, and some were not reading at all. "I told you to read together," Keniesha said over and over again. "We are," was the common response. When it came time to answer the questions, it got even worse. At every group, she noticed one person doing all the thinking and working, while others sat silently, nodding their heads. "What do they not understand about the word 'together'?" Keniesha wondered for the umpteenth time. She knew the only way she could really assess everyone's understanding was to have them work independently.

A Student's Perspective

"Oh great," thought Darius, rolling his eyes. "I'm in a group with Dawn again!" Every time they worked in a group, it was the same old thing. Dawn took over and there was nothing left to do. Then, inevitably Ms. Glover would get on to them for not working together. Darius had told her before that Dawn was doing all the work and he had nothing to do, but Ms. Glover just told him not to let her do that. Easier said than done! "Oh, well," thought Darius, "here we go again."

WHAT IS COLLABORATION AND HOW IS IT DIFFERENT FROM GROUP WORK?

Ms. Glover has a very common misconception: that collaboration and group work are synonymous. Many believe that by telling students to "work together," something magical will happen. However, those of us who have tried this have had similar experiences to Ms. Glover, and our students end up either feeling frustrated like Darius because one student takes over the task while the others are pushed out, or overwhelmed if they are the student who feels they need to take on the whole project, or they are elated because this provides the opportunity to "hitchhike" along for ride.

So how are group work and collaboration different? (See below.) According to Kagan and Kagan (2009), "simply giving a task to a group

	Group work	Collaboration
Purpose	Working together on a common task	Working together on a common task
Goal	To complete a task together	To deepen thinking so learning becomes richer and more meaningful
Structure	No imposed structure	Structure is provided to ensure equal and productive participation by all group members.
Student Roles	Roles in the task are not defined and/or not directly correlated to the learning objective	Roles are clearly defined, equally important, and require deep manipulation of the content.
Teacher Role	Manager	Facilitator
What the Students Are Saying	"I never get to do anything." "I always have to do everything."	"We all need to do our part so that we are successful."
What the Teacher Is Saying	"Why aren't you working together?"	"Andy, you are the synthesizer. What do you need in order to guide your group in creating a summary of the lesson?"

with no structuring or roles is group work." For a task to be truly collaborative, there must be a structure in place that ensures that each member of the group is equally productive during the task and is fully accountable for the content being learned. The goal of any collaborative task is that through the process of collaborating, thinking is deepened, the learning becomes richer and more meaningful, and the task itself is more engaging for all students.

Ms. Glover asked her students to read the story together. Based on her observations, that was interpreted many different ways and Ms. Glover had no real task for which to hold the students accountable. To make this more collaborative, Ms. Glover could assign students specific jobs to do during the reading. For example, one student could create questions about the story, one student could explain how the illustrations support the text, one student could capture words and phrases that bring the story to life, and so on. Everyone is responsible for an important role in analyzing the text while it is being read. The same principle holds true when students are answering questions.

This chapter contains eight strategies for collaboration that provide structures to ensure that all students are participating fully and equally in the learning tasks and are held accountable for the content being learned.

WHY IT WORKS

Keniesha Glover did what all of us as teachers have done at some point in our teaching career. Her principal wanted students collaborating, so she put them together and told them to "get to work." The problem is, as was told by Ms. Glover and Darius, the students thought they *were* working together. What Ms. Glover and her students failed to understand is "group work" is not synonymous with "collaboration."

Learning is a social process. As Tony Wagner states in his book, *The Global Achievement Gap*, "isolation is the enemy of improvement" (2008). In order for our students to be college- and career-ready, an academic atmosphere that promotes collaboration must be apparent in our classrooms. What does that really mean? The critical difference in the terms "group work" and "collaboration" is that collaboration provides a specific structure for ensuring all students within a small group (group of 2, 3, or 4) have specific responsibilities related to the completion of the task and all students are held accountable individually for successful completion of their specific part of the task (Kagan & Kagan, 2009). Group work simply asks that students "get together and get to work," thus ensuring nothing meaningful is being accomplished other than what Darius shared about Dawn "doing all of the work."

According to research studies conducted by Johnson and Johnson (2009), collaboration, when used effectively, improves student engagement and retention of classroom material, as well as improves students' time on task and motivation to learn, and students' interpersonal relationships and expectations for personal success are increased. When students are encouraged to reach out to each other to solve problems and share knowledge in a cohesive manner, it not only deepens their understanding of how collaboration looks, sounds, and feels, but it also leads to a richer and more meaningful learning experience that improves comprehension and critical-thinking skills for all students.

STRATEGIES FOR COLLABORATION

PARTNER READING

Keniesha Glover was asked by her administrator to make learning collaborative, and that's exactly what she tried to do over and over again—but it always ended in frustration because she could not get her students to actually *do* collaboration. The problem wasn't that her students could not work together; the problem was that her students didn't have a mental picture of what working together should look, sound, and feel like. They needed a structure and without it, Dawn would continue to dominate group work time no matter the group she was with.

Ms. Glover needed a collaborative strategy such as Partner Reading. The structure that Partner Reading creates would eliminate Darius' negativity about having to work with Dawn again. Ms. Glover could have begun by purposefully and intentionally partnering her students to ensure appropriate challenge and work between the partners. Once partner groups have been established, students are equipped to then productively progress through the learning task with a clear picture of what is expected. In Partner Reading, students determine who will be Partner A and who will be Partner B. Then they are given specific roles to ensure both partners are equally contributing and participating. In Ms. Glover's scenario, she could ask Partner A to be the reader for the first chunk of text and ask Partner B to follow along and be prepared to summarize what was read by Partner A. This ensures each student has an active role in learning. If she had implemented Partner Reading, then Darius would have no complaints because Dawn wouldn't be able to "take over" as she normally does.

Partner Reading

Preparation: Choose how you want students to interact with the reading task and embed that structure within the procedure for students.

Time Needed: 10–60 minutes (depending on grade level and reading task)

Grouping: 2 students per group

Procedures for Students:

1. Divide the text into logical chunks.

2. Determine who will be Partner A and Partner B.

3. Partner A begins by reading the first chunk while Partner B follows along and summarizes what Partner A read.

4. Switch roles for the next part so that Partner B is reading the second chunk and Partner A follows along and summarizes what Partner B read.

5. Continue this process until the reading task has been completed.

Suggested Adaptations:

- Partnering stronger students with struggling readers will enable both students to access complex texts together.

- The roles of each partner could be changed to address the needs of students.

Working in partner groups is effective because those students struggling to connect with others, who steer clear of working with others, and who don't have—what they think—are the skills needed to participate productively, find that Partner Reading lessens their anxiety and they contribute more because they are working with one peer. In their minds, this is a "doable" process and empowers them to become a more engaged and active learner.

TURNABOUT TEACHING

I think the Greek philosopher Aristotle states it best: "Teaching is the highest form of understanding." If we, as educators, believe in this philosophy, then we must put students in a position to teach others often. That is the goal of the collaborative strategy called Turnabout Teaching.

Keniesha Glover's students were told to work together to read a story and answer the questions at the end of it. A vague statement like this will always lead to a "Dawn dilemma" because students will do what they *think* is the right way of doing which, nine times out of 10, involves one person doing all the work while everyone else takes credit for what is turned in for a grade. What if, however, Keniesha had asked her students to read the story for a specific purpose, such as the following:

Read pages 89–93 and determine a theme from details in the text, including how the two main characters responded to the challenges they faced.

Once students completed the task, their job would be to teach a partner what they determined the theme to be based on evidence from the story and how the two main characters responded to the challenges faced based on this theme. In this scenario, there is no one right answer to theme, which is why Turnabout Teaching would work so well. Each student teaches his or her partner differently based on the theme identified and the challenges determined.

Classroom Close-up:
Turnabout Teaching

I wanted my band and orchestra students to have frequent opportunities for meaningful practice and immediate, individualized feedback, but there were so many of them and only one of me! I used Turnabout Teaching as a way to make this happen. I grouped my students in pairs for partner practice and feedback. One student (Partner A) played part of a piece of music while the other student (Partner B) listened and followed along on the sheet music. Partner B would then give Partner A specific feedback using sentence frames I provided. Partner A would play the piece again implementing the feedback he or she had received. They would take turns until both students felt they had reached a level of mastery. At that point they would let me know that they were ready to be assessed by me. Not only did students achieve mastery more quickly, they also remained actively engaged throughout the class period.

—Christina Randall,
middle-school band teacher,
Hardeeville, SC

Turnabout Teaching works because it places both students in the role of teacher. It's important to note that this strategy isn't called Turnabout Telling. If we want our students to actually learn *how* to teach, then they need to know *what* that really is. Modeling and practice of this strategy is critical in order to get the biggest bang for your buck. Once students understand they are not telling their partners but teaching them, this strategy has the power to be one of the most essential and well used of your instructional toolbox.

Turnabout Teaching

Preparation: Determine a meaningful learning task for students to attend to as they follow through to ensure they are equipped with something intentional to teach another student.

Time Needed: 10–45 minutes (depending on grade level)

Grouping: Pairs

Procedures for Students:

1. Complete the learning task.

2. Get with a partner and teach him or her the goal of the learning task.

3. Switch roles to ensure both partners have an opportunity to teach.

Suggested Adaptations:

- Provide sentence frames for younger students and special education students to ensure needed supports are given so students are successful.

COLLABORATION CAROUSEL

Once Ms. Glover put collaborative structures in place, she was amazed by how powerful collaboration was for student learning. She is at the end of a unit and wants to provide a review, but she doesn't want it to be the typical sit-and-get or fill-in-the-blank study sheets she had used in the past. She wants students thinking critically and collaborating to share information about what they learned. This is the perfect opportunity for a Collaboration Carousel.

A Collaboration Carousel provides a structure for students to rotate through various tasks, processing content in a variety of ways. Ms. Glover chose Pass the Buck, Turnabout Teaching, Partner Reading, and Interactive Worksheet as the collaborative stations she wanted students to participate in to review what they learned. She printed out procedures for each station and set up two sets of each station. Students were divided into groups of four and rotated through each of the four stations. The review of content was completely self-directed and student-driven, and gave students the opportunity to review the content in a variety of different ways. As students visited each station, they were also building a study guide that could be taken home for further study and review.

Collaboration Carousel does not only have to be used as a review. Questions can be posted at each station, and small groups of students rotate through each question adding information, providing additional evidence, and expanding on responses of previous groups. Another application of Collaboration Carousel is to post topics at each station and allow students to rotate through, generating questions about the topics on the first round, and responding to the questions other groups posted on the second round. This strategy can also be used to facilitate student-driven small group discussions by posting procedures for various strategies for academic dialogue (see Chapter 3).

Collaboration Carousel

Preparation: Print out written procedures for each carousel station and prepare any materials or resources for each. If desired, prepare a study sheet that can be partially completed at each station based on the information reviewed at that station.

Time Needed: Depends on the number of stations and length of task at each station

Grouping: Groups of 4

Procedures for Students for Carousel Review:

1. With your group, read the procedures for your station.

2. Participate in the task at your station until time is called.

3. Compare the section of your study sheet for that station with other group members to ensure that everyone has it filled in accurately and comprehensively.

4. When directed, rotate to the next station.

5. Continue until you have completed all stations.

Suggested Adaptations:

- For younger students, provide only two stations to rotate through.
- In math, ask students to use a different problem-solving strategy at each station.
- In English Language Arts, review different literacry devices or portions of text at each station.

EXPERT JIGSAW

In the Expert Jigsaw process (Aronson & Patnoe, 2011), students are encouraged to be active listeners, mentally engaged, and empathetic by giving each member of the group an essential part to play in the learning task. Group members must work together as a team to accomplish a common goal; each person depends on all the others. No student can succeed completely unless everyone works well together as a team. This "cooperation by design" facilitates interaction among all students in the class, leading them to value each other as contributors to their common task.

Let's take a closer look at Ms. Glover's classroom. What if she had used the Expert Jigsaw strategy with her students? What would it look like? She wanted her students to work together to read the story and answer the questions at the end of it. Suppose she chunked the text into four equal parts, such as this:

1st Chunk: read pages 89–92

2nd Chunk: read pages 93–96

3rd Chunk: read pages 97–100

4th Chunk: read pages 101–104

Then she asked each collaborative group (aka, home group) to determine who would read each chunk. Once determined, students would leave their home group and meet with others from other collaborative groups who are reading the same chunk of text (aka, expert group). Once in an expert group, students are given specific roles (see below) as they read and complete a connected learning task. An example of this could be that students in their expert groups read to find out what information in the text tells them more about the challenges faced by the two main characters. Now that they have a very specific task to complete as they read, they are equipped to do so productively because they are mentally engaged in reading for a purpose. For example, Ms. Glover could have used the following roles as students worked in expert groups:

Text Evidence Detective: When you hear information that answers today's question, say "Stop!" and give everyone a chance to flag/highlight the information in the text.

Close Reading Director: Uses the Oral Cloze Routine and reads the text aloud while other group members follow along in their own texts and holds all group members accountable for participation.

Synthesizer: Uses the flagged/highlighted information to write a complete and concise answer to the question after the group comes to consensus.

Once expert groups complete their assigned task, they return to their home groups and share. Now Ms. Glover has tackled a long text effectively, and her students engaged collaboratively through the structure of Expert Jigsaw.

The Expert Jigsaw strategy places great emphasis on cooperation and shared responsibility within groups (Aronson, Blaney, Stephin, & Snapp, 1978). The success of each group depends on the participation of each individual in completing their task. This means the strategy effectively increases the involvement of each student in the activity, thus helping students like Darius feel empowered and successful as they equally participate in the process.

Classroom Close-up: Expert Jigsaw

The challenge of teaching history is that there is so much to teach and not enough time to get it all in. Using Expert Jigsaw has provided a way to go deeper with a large amount of content. I put my students in groups of three and gave each group three different articles from three different perspectives about World War II. Each student would get together with others who had the same article. They would then read and annotate the article together. I then asked them to create interview questions to ask someone who had a different article to try to get that perspective about the war. Students would then return to their original group of three and take turns interviewing each other to get all three perspectives of the war. Once they had all three perspectives, students used this information to write a compare/contrast essay. Using the Expert Jigsaw instead of just having students do everything individually allowed us to get more done and go deeper in our thinking.

—Russell Kusaka, high school social studies teacher, Waialua, HI

Expert Jigsaw

Preparation: Determine how you want to divide the task students will be completing in their expert groups, develop roles for the expert groups to ensure goals are met, and model and practice what it should look, sound, and feel like in these groups ahead of time.

(Continued)

(Continued)

Time Needed: 15–45 minutes (depending on the age of the student and the complexity of the task)

Grouping: 3–4 students per group

Procedures for Students:

1. In your home learning group, decide who will complete the assigned sections of the learning task.

2. Meet with your expert group in the designated area of the classroom.

3. Using your assigned roles, complete the learning task with your expert group.

4. When time is called, return to your home group and share your work.

Suggested Adaptations:

- If reading is involved, struggling readers can be paired with a stronger reader and they can complete the task together.

- Expert Jigsaw can be used with anything you are using in your classroom that can be chunked into smaller pieces for students to complete.

- Related arts teachers can use Expert Jigsaw with artwork, with physical education skills, with music concepts, and with computer skills.

GROUP ROLES

Many students can relate to Darius' frustration knowing he is in a group with Dawn, who always takes over. Darius has told Ms. Glover the problem, but neither can see a tangible solution. What Darius is really asking Ms. Glover to do is assign group roles. Group roles define the specific task or job each student will complete in order to accomplish the larger collaborative assignment.

For group roles to be effective and for the task to be truly collaborative, each role must be equally significant and each student must walk away from the task having deeply processed the content of the assignment. While roles like timekeeper and materials manager can be helpful, they cannot serve as a student's only role in the assignment because neither requires that the student think deeply about the content or be held accountable for learning the information.

Group roles should be designed to fit the objective of the assignment, and job descriptions for roles should be posted in writing for students to refer to as they work on the assignment.

The size of the group should be determined by the number of roles needed to complete the assignment effectively. Groups of two to four usually work best.

Some suggestions for group roles:

Discussion Leader: Lead a discussion about what has been learned about the topic and make sure all group members are actively involved in the discussion. After a person has shared, clarify what they have said by saying, "What I heard you say was _____."

Text Detective: Find information in the text to support or justify the responses to the question or topic.

Graphic Features Analyst: Study photos, illustrations, charts, and/or graphs and explain how they support the information in the text.

Questioner: Create questions for the group or to ask other groups about the content.

Summarizer: Summarize the discussion into bulleted points.

Synthesizer: Lead the group in synthesizing the discussion into a "statement of insight" of what you learned and record it.

Artist: Create a picture or symbol to illustrate your statement of insight.

Reporter: Share your group's statement of insight with the whole group, explain how your group came up with it, and respond to questions from the class.

Group Roles

Preparation: Create and post job descriptions for each group role.

Time Needed: Varies based on the complexity of the collaborative task

Grouping: 2–4, based on the roles needed to complete the task

Procedures for Students:

1. Read the job descriptions for each of the group roles.

2. Briefly discuss with your group your plan for completing this task effectively.

(Continued)

(Continued)

3. When you have completed the task, go back and reread the roles to ensure that each group member is accountable for his or her role in the task.

Suggested Adaptations:

- When first using group roles, start with groups of two so that the task is less overwhelming for both teacher and students.

- For math tasks, consider having one student set up the problem in writing two different ways, another student explains one way of solving it, the third student explains an alternate way of solving it.

- For gifted students, give them the task and let them create their own roles and descriptions for the roles.

PASS THE BUCK

Another strategy Ms. Glover could have used with her students to ensure she was following Dr. Johnson's recommendation of implementing collaboration is Pass the Buck.

Pass the Buck works well for any subject and any grade level. The teacher determines four open-ended questions that would elicit meaningful responses from students. Each question is then placed on a sheet of paper so there would be four sheets of paper in all for each group of four students. Once the teacher explains the process using the attached procedure, students begin the task. They work on answering the question on the sheet of paper in front of them until they hear the timer ring. Then they pass their paper with their answer to the person next to them clockwise (pass the "buck"). Now everyone in the group has a new question to answer but they must read what is already written and add to that response, create a new response, or respond to someone else's response. When the timer rings, students pass their papers clockwise and the process is repeated. This continues until all four of the group members receive their original papers. Students then read all of the responses, analyze to identify trends in all of the answers, and create a summary statement (one sentence) that captures a complete and concise answer to the question. This task ends with students standing in a Group Huddle (see p. 35) as each student reads his or her summary statement to the other group members. By the time Pass the Buck has been completed, students feel accomplished and the teacher feels less anxious because so much has been done in a short amount of time.

This strategy is naturally differentiated to meet the needs of all learners—struggling to gifted—because it gives the struggling learners appropriate mental models of how it looks, sounds, and feels to answer a question concisely and completely. It forces the "just let me do the minimum" students to think deeper because by the time the paper has reached the second and third person, the simplistic answer has already been written. It works perfectly for the gifted students because it gives them an avenue to think and write as much as they want to or can in the allotted time given to answer the question.

What could this look like in Ms. Glover's room with students like Dawn and Darius? She asked students to read and answer the questions at the end of the story. What if she used those questions or came up with some of her own as her Pass the Buck questions? Let's take a closer look.

1. *What do you think the theme is in this story, and what makes you think this?*

2. *What is significant about how the main characters respond to challenges throughout the story?*

3. *What advice would you give the main characters to ensure they don't make the same mistakes again?*

4. *Based on what you know about the main characters, how would you describe them?*

Classroom Close-up: Pass the Buck

Pass the Buck is a great collaborative strategy because it requires engagement from every student—from the highest achiever in the room to the one who always struggles. For my World History class, I come up with four big, open-ended questions about the content we are studying. I write each question at the top of a piece of paper and make a set of questions for each group of four students. Students write a response to the question on the paper in front of them. I usually give them 2 or 3 minutes depending on the depth of the question and whether they will need to refer to their textbook or class notes for their response. When the timer buzzes, students pass their papers and read their new question and whatever responses are written. They can write their own answer, comment on someone else's answer, or—the aspect I like best—add to an existing answer. This really takes the pressure off the lower-performing students to think of something different. When students get back the paper with the first question they answered, they read all responses and summarize them. Sometimes this is done orally and sometimes it is done in writing. All summaries are shared in small groups, giving all students a chance to hear what each answer turned in to after everyone had a chance to work on it.

—Lauren Levin, high school social studies teacher, Atlanta, GA

When Ms. Glover sets up the learning task to look like the above, students like Dawn and Darius get their needs met and are happy, productive students.

Pass the Buck

Preparation: Choose three or four ideas, questions, prompts, pictures, and so on and type them onto the sheets of paper ahead of time.

Time Needed: 5–10 minutes (depending on age of student and Pass the Buck prompts)

Grouping: 3–4 students per group

Procedures for Students:

1. Read or look at the prompt, picture, photo, and so on.

2. Think about your response and record information about it until time is called.

3. When prompted, pass your paper to the next person in your group (clockwise).

4. Repeat these steps until you have your original paper back.

5. Look over your paper and determine trends.

6. Create a summary statement that captures your group's thinking.

7. Participate in a Group Huddle to share with your learning group.

Suggested Adaptations:

- Can be used to activate prior knowledge at the beginning of class, used during guided practice, and used as closure at the end of lessons.

- Younger students can participate by using pictures, letters, and so on to play.

- Related arts teachers adapt the prompts by using their specific academic content.

INTERACTIVE WORKSHEET

Instead of asking students to "work together" to answer the questions at the end of the story, Ms. Glover could have taken the task from group work to collaboration by using an interactive worksheet. She could type the questions on to a worksheet and ask students to cut them into strips. She would then give each group of four a clean worksheet. Students in each group would pair up and each pair would choose a question strip to complete. Once both pairs were finished with their questions, they would trade. After the pairs finished the second question, they compare and contrast their answers to both questions, evaluating them to ensure they are as clear and comprehensive as possible. Next, they devise a consensus response to each question that is written on the clean group worksheet. They continue this process until all questions are answered or time is called. During this time, Ms. Glover is free to check in with pairs and listen to group conversations, formatively assessing and reteaching as necessary.

The Interactive Worksheet strategy can be used with any worksheet in any content area. What makes it collaborative is that all students are participating equally and the final response is deeper, richer, and more precise than if students had worked on the question or problem individually.

Interactive Worksheet

Preparation: Make two copies of worksheet for each group of 4.

Time Needed: Depends on the length and complexity of the worksheet

Grouping: Groups of 4 that split up into pairs

Procedures for Students:

1. Form a group of four and then divide into pairs.

2. Cut one of the worksheets into strips.

3. Place strips in the center of your work area.

4. Each pair chooses a strip and answers the question.

5. Switch strip with the other pair and answer that question.

6. Once both pairs have answered the same two questions, compare and contrast your answers and come to a consensus about how to most clearly communicate your answer.

7. Choose one of you to write the consensus response on the clean worksheet.

8. Continue until all strips have been completed or until time is called.

Suggested Adaptations:

- For younger or special needs students, the teacher can precut the worksheets.

- In math, pairs would compare and contrast explanations of how they solved the problems in order to come to a consensus explanation.

- To differentiate, modify the number of strips or the complexity of the worksheet.

- In physical education, art, music, and so on, create strips with content-specific questions or tasks.

TWITTERFEST

Instead of just answering the questions at the end of the story, Ms. Glover could have had a Twitterfest. She could write each of the open-ended, inferential, and opinion questions on a separate sheet of chart paper and place them on tables with markers. Students would divide into groups of four and determine who will be the discussion leader, summarizer, tweeter, and responder. As students rotate from question to question, instead of just writing their responses, they discuss each question in depth, summarize the main points of their discussion, and synthesize these points into a statement of 140 characters or less. Students then have the opportunity to get in on the thinking of students outside their group when they read and respond to the tweets that have already been posted. All students are actively involved in the process of thinking about, discussing, and responding to each question as they complete the task assigned to their specific role during that round.

Twitterfest

Preparation: Write questions or topics on sheets of chart paper (one per group); provide markers for each table; visual timer.

Time Needed: 25–30 minutes

Grouping: Groups of 4

Procedures for Students:

1. Form a group of four and assign the following roles: discussion leader, summarizer, tweeter, and responder. (You will rotate these roles during the Twitterfest.)

2. Discussion leader will lead the group in discussing the table topic for four minutes.

3. When the timer sounds, the summarizer will give the group a verbal summary of what has been discussed.

4. The tweeter will lead the group in turning the summary into a tweet or tweets (140 characters or less) and will post it on the chart paper under your trending topic.

5. Turn your Twitter feed over, and rotate tables when directed.

6. Switch roles.

7. Discussion leader will lead a discussion of the new table topic with your group for four minutes, followed by an oral summary given by the summarizer.

8. When directed, the responder will read the Twitter feed and will lead the group in responding, liking, retweeting, and/or adding emojis to any post.

9. Tweeter will add your own post.

10. Turn your Twitter feed over, and rotate tables when directed.

11. Continue this process until you are back at your original table, rotating roles each time.

12. Discussion leader will lead a discussion on the feed for your topic.

13. Summarizer will create a brief verbal summary.

14. Responder will share the summary with the group.

Suggested Adaptations:

- If you only have a few questions or topics to discuss, you can have two or three rotations going simultaneously, discussing the same questions/topics.

- Give students index cards with the roles printed on them to help them keep track of who is responsible for each job each round.

- Younger children can tweet an image by summarizing their discussion into a picture.

- Younger children or special needs students can share their tweets verbally and, after one group shares, groups can collaborate on a response and share it verbally.

- Art, physical education, and music students can tweet about works of art, songs, games or exercises, and so on.

Questions for Reflection

1. After reading this chapter, how has your thinking changed about collaboration?

2. Which collaborative strategy are you willing to try first and why?

3. Change the following tasks from group work to collaboration:

    a Work on problems 1–10 together.

    b Read Chapter 3 with a partner.

    c With your group, answer the questions at the end of the section of your textbook.

5 Get Moving

Embedding Purposeful
Movement Into Instruction

VIGNETTES

A Teacher's Perspective

Sherry Paulk sighed as her last class of seventh graders left for the day. What had gone wrong? She had been especially excited about today's lesson. She had found a great video clip the night before and couldn't wait to discuss it with her students. Things started out fine, and her students genuinely seemed interested in the lesson, but after 10 or 15 minutes, everything started going downhill. Terrance got up to throw something in the trash can, and that must have seemed like a good idea, because suddenly five or six others needed to throw something away, too. Before she could ask everyone to remain in their seats, Travis fell out of his chair and she noticed two students nodding off in the back. Before the bell rang, those two were completely asleep and three others were well on their way. How could they possibly sleep through this lesson that she had so artfully planned and was so passionate about? What do you have to do to keep kids' attention these days?

A Student's Perspective

Terrance closed his locker as he headed to his last class for the day. He liked Ms. Paulk. She was pretty cool and told really good stories. She usually showed a video clip or played a song to go with what she was teaching.

Terrance knew he got on her nerves, though. She always gave him "the look" when he got out of his seat to throw something in the trash. He couldn't help it . . . his rear end hurt after sitting in those desks all day. At least he didn't fall asleep. Maybe if Gina and James would make an occasional trip to the trash can, they could stay awake, too.

WHAT IS PURPOSEFUL MOVEMENT?

We have all been in Ms. Paulk's shoes: a beautifully planned lesson that we are passionate about falls flat after 10 or 15 minutes. How can students get out of their seats and fall out of their chairs when we are being brilliant? It is because what we are asking of them is in direct contradiction to what human beings are designed to do. What are the two things a healthy baby does when he is born? He cries and moves. What are the first two things we ask children to when they come to school? Stay in their seats and be quiet. Human beings are wired for movement (Ratey, 2008), and they will create movement for themselves when it is not provided.

There are teachers who are cognizant of this need and take steps to provide for it. Some give students stretch breaks, others provide opportunities for students to "get the wiggles out" through dances and games. Some provide time for students to work in centers, rotating from place to place in the classroom. So what is purposeful movement and how is it different? The word "purposeful" implies that there is intention behind the movement. It has been planned in advance for a specific reason. Purposeful movement utilizes an instructional strategy that allows students to move while processing content. It is directly connected with learning and enhances instruction instead of detracting or breaking from it.

Let's take Ms. Paulk's situation. When she became aware that her students needed movement, she had a couple of choices. She could stop her lesson, give everyone a chance to stand and stretch, and then resume instruction. She is providing the movement her students need, but she has used precious class time for a non-instructional activity and then uses more time to backpedal in order to refocus her students on the lesson. Her other option is to implement an instructional strategy that embeds movement into learning. This purposeful movement becomes part of her instruction and primes students for what's next. With instructional time at a premium, purposeful movement makes every minute count. This chapter will discuss the research and benefits of providing movement in the classroom and will include eight instructional strategies for embedding movement meaningfully and intentionally into lessons.

WHY IT WORKS

Have you ever sat in a staff meeting or in a professional development training for a long period of time and noticed the behaviors of others around you: legs bouncing up and down, fingers thumping on the tables, or backs being stretched? These are all signs of restlessness. Then the trainer gives everyone a break and what do you do? Jump up, walk around the room, go to the restroom, get a snack—anything that will re-energize your body and brain. This opportunity to move helped reset your emotional state to one of alertness and gave you a burst of renewed energy (Ratey, 2002). Students in classrooms across the country experience the same mental fatigue day in and day out without options, other than walking to a trashcan to throw away a microscopic piece of paper as Terrance did in our vignette at the beginning of the chapter.

According to research conducted by Galen Cranz (2000), "sitting in chairs for more than brief 10-minute intervals reduces our awareness of physical and emotional sensations and increases fatigue." In the classroom, these challenges will eventually lead to lack of focused attention and ability to learn, less thinking and productivity, and behavior challenges—all of which are detrimental to today's achievement expectations and requirements. Embedding purposeful movement structures and strategies into daily lessons will provide the essential anchors from which thinking and learning can evolve. In his book, *Spark*, Dr. John Ratey states, "the latest research shows that for your brain to function at its peak, your body needs to move" (2008). Optimal cognitive functioning depends on this understanding. The release of endorphins, peptides secreted within the brain and nervous system, during the use of purposeful movement-based tasks creates feelings of pleasure, satisfaction, and a positive sense of well-being. As Dr. Carla Hannaford states in her book *Smart Moves*, "movement activates the neural wiring throughout the entire body, making the whole body the instrument of learning" (2007).

Creating this mindset will require intentional and purposeful planning, however, the pay-off will be creating opportunities for students to go from "sitters and getters" to "doers and thinkers."

STRATEGIES FOR EMBEDDING PURPOSEFUL MOVEMENT

STAND UP, HAND UP, PAIR UP

Stand Up, Hand Up, Pair Up, from Dr. Spencer Kagan (Kagan & Kagan, 2009), is an ideal strategy for Ms. Paulk to use because it requires no preparation and allows her to provide both a mental and physical "shift" when she senses her students are "checking out." She had captured her students' attention with a brief video clip, and they needed both the opportunity to process what they saw and to get up and move. After or during the video Ms. Paulk could ask students to jot down three things that they want to remember. Taking their "jots," the students stand up, put a hand up, find a partner and give that person a "high five." Partners take turns sharing the first thing they wrote down, then hands go up again as they look for a new partner to share the second idea. This process continues until students have shared all three things they wrote, and then they sit down. At this point, the brains of every student in the classroom are buzzing with ideas about the video and they are primed and ready for Ms. Paulk to open up a discussion or provide some direct instruction.

The prompt for Stand Up, Hand Up, Pair Up (Kagan & Kagan, 2009) can be as general or specific as is needed for the lesson. It can be a specific question that students respond to and share their response with two or three people, or it can be an open-ended reflection of learning, like Ms. Paulk's prompt. Asking students to write their responses first is not required, but it provides more focus to students' discussion.

Posting the prompt and the procedures for Stand Up, Hand Up, Pair Up (Kagan & Kagan, 2009) allows students to be more productive and self-directed, and allows the teacher to be more of a facilitator, rather than having to repeat instructions and verbally redirect students. When the teacher is able to listen in on the students' academic conversations, he or she can use these as a springboard for instruction or class discussion. This also becomes an effective tool for formative assessment, giving the teacher a snapshot of where the students are and where to take them next.

Classroom Close-Up:
Stand Up, Hand Up, Pair Up

Keeping my junior and senior special education students actively engaged for a 74-minute block is a challenge. I found that if I chunked up my instruction into smaller pieces that only lasted about 15 minutes I could hold their attention. Following that 15 minutes learning segment I wanted students to do something with what I had taught. Stand Up, Hand Up, Pair Up is one of their favorite ways to talk about what they learned. I give students a question about what was learned during that chunk of instruction and they write their answer on an index card. Then they stand up, put their hand up, and find someone to give a high five. They take turns talking about what they wrote, then they put their hands up and do the same thing again. Once they've done this a few times, they return to their seats and are ready for the next chunk. This also gives me an opportunity to see who knows what and what I really need to focus on during my next piece of instruction. One insight I have gained through using this strategy is that my students are much more apt to give evidence to support their thinking when they are discussing with a peer than when we are discussing as a whole class.
—Sheryl Almeida, high school special education teacher, Waialua, HI

Stand Up, Hand Up, Pair Up

Preparation: No preparation is required.

Time Needed: 8–10 minutes

Grouping: Pairs

Procedures for Students:

1. Write your response to the prompt.

2. When directed, stand up, put your hand up, pair up with a student who does not sit near you, and give a high five.

3. Take turns sharing your first response to the prompt.

4. When finished, put your hand up and pair up with a different student with his or her hand up.

5. Take turns sharing your second response.

6. Repeat this process until you have shared all three responses.

7. Return to your seat when finished.

Suggested Adaptations and Applications to Other Content Areas:

- Very young children can draw a response and share their thinking with their partners.

- If there is very limited space to move, students can stand and share with the person in front, behind, to the left, to the right, and so on.

- If time is limited, the number of times students pair up can be reduced to one or two.

- Suggested uses in English language arts: share a writing piece as it goes through the various stages of the writing process; write and discuss the character, setting, plot, and theme of a story

- Suggested uses in mathematics: share and explain the strategy you used to solve the math problem

- Suggested uses in science: create a diagram to show a scientific process and Stand Up, Hand Up, Pair Up to share and discuss; write conclusions you drew from the lab and Stand Up, Hand Up, Pair Up to compare with others

- Suggested uses in social studies: write and share the most important thing that was learned that day; find locations on a map and Stand Up, Hand Up, Pair Up to discuss and compare

(Continued)

(Continued)

- Suggested uses in physical education/music/art: Respond to questions about skills learned in physical education, music, or art and discuss with a partner; Stand Up, Hand Up, Pair Up to share application of the skill and provide feedback

Source: This material has been adapted with permission from Kagan Publishing & Professional Development from the following book: Kagan, Spencer & Kagan, Miguel. *Kagan Cooperative Learning*. San Clemente, CA: Kagan Publishing, 2009. 1 (800) 933-2667. www.KaganOnline.com.

FIND YOUR MATCH

Ms. Paulk really wants to add purposeful movement to her lesson, but she wants more control over the pairing of her students than Stand Up, Hand Up, Pair Up offers. She has allowed her students to pair themselves before, and found that sometimes two students who struggle academically end up together, and that other students tend to stick to pairing with only their friends. She has assigned partners in the past, but that was not met with the same excitement and enthusiasm as random pairing. Find Your Match is an effective strategy to meet Ms. Paulk's needs and to engage her students.

Ms. Paulk has prepared a special deck of playing cards to use in Find Your Match. The deck is made up of cards from two different decks and is comprised of pairs of the same card (two sixes of diamonds, two kings of spades, etc.) After showing the video at the beginning of her lesson, Ms. Paulk asked the students to jot down three things they learned. She then distributes a card to each student, making sure that if she gives one king of spades to a struggling student, she gives the other to a higher achiever; if she gives Terrance a six of diamonds, the other six of diamonds will not go to his best friend, because they tend to get off topic when they are partners. Once every student has a card, they are instructed to find their matches and discuss what they learned.

Classroom Close-Up:
Find Your Match

I had two goals: I knew my students needed opportunities to get up out of their seats, and I wanted to engage them in the lesson before I started my instruction. Find Your Match allowed me to meet both those goals. We were studying the American Revolution and were about to begin learning about the causes of the Revolutionary War. We were beginning with the Tea Act, and I wanted to spark the students' thinking around this. I had gotten a variety pack of individually wrapped tea bags and took out two of each kind. I gave each a tea bag and asked them to find their match

Playing cards are just one thing that can be matched. Younger students enjoy matching pictures of items that go together, such as peanut butter and jelly or shoes and socks. Colored index cards that have been numbered can also be used. If students are tempted to trade cards in order to be with a friend, they can be further randomized. By putting a shape, a letter, and a number on colored index cards, teachers have three options for pairing students.

Objects used to pair students can also be catalysts for discussion. For example, if the teacher wants students to brainstorm words that begin with a certain letter, the match can be a capital and lowercase letter. If teachers want students to discuss specific characters in a story, the characters' names can provide the match.

(the person who had the same kind of tea bag as them.) Once they were matched up, students discussed the question, "What do you think tea has to do with the Revolutionary War?" After their discussion, students returned to their seats and couldn't wait to find out what tea and the Revolutionary War had in common. The best part was after they learned about the Tea Act, they could take their tea bags home and share with their family what they had learned.

—Tarsha Wingfield, fourth-grade teacher, Columbia, SC

Find Your Match

Preparation: Objects or cards to match need to be prepared and counted to ensure the right number is ready for each group of students.

Time Needed: 8–10 minutes

Grouping: Pairs

Procedures for Students:

1. Write your response to the prompt.

2. When directed, find your match.

3. Take turns sharing your response to the prompt.

4. Return to your seat when finished.

Suggested Adaptations and Applications to Other Content Areas:

- Have a "wild card" ready if there is an uneven number of students. If using playing cards, add in a Joker. The student who gets the Joker can choose to join any pair to make a group of three.

(Continued)

(Continued)

- Find Your Match doesn't have to be limited to pairs. Create the number of matches for the number of students you want in a group.
- Suggested uses in English language arts: possible items to match include contractions, vocabulary words, synonyms/antonyms, words with same number of syllables
- Suggested uses in mathematics: possible items to match include evens and odds, two-dimensional and three-dimensional shapes, corresponding commutative property, inverse operation, missing variable
- Suggested uses in science: half the students have real-world items (e.g., jewelry, cleaning products) and the other half have an element from the periodic table and students find one of the elements contained in their item; find the person with the same scientific tool and/or item that you have and discuss how you think it will be used in today's lab
- Suggested uses in social studies: match a picture card of a historical figure with his or her contribution to history; match country cards with continent cards
- Suggested use in physical education: distribute cards with muscle groups and exercises and ask students to find the exercise that uses their muscle group or vice versa
- Suggested use for music: distribute music flash cards and ask students to find the student who has the letter that matches the musical note on a scale
- Suggested applications for art: give out primary color paint chips and ask students to match up with someone holding a different colored chip and discuss what secondary color they make together

MINGLE TO MUSIC

Ms. Paulk has tried both Stand Up, Hand Up, Pair Up (Kagan & Kagan, 2009) and Find Your Match with her students and likes aspects of both strategies. She appreciates the fact that Stand Up, Hand Up, Pair Up allows her students to pair up more than once, and that it requires no preparation. With Find Your Match, Ms. Paulk likes the fact that she is able to manage the amount of time her students are engaged in discussion to help make sure that they stay on topic. Mingle to Music is a great option for Ms. Paulk because it contains the elements that work best for her and her students.

Ms. Paulk is halfway through her lesson and wants her students to discuss what she has taught, but she knows they need to move and also wants to be sure that all students are actively involved in the discussion. She turns on some music and her students walk silently throughout the classroom. When the music stops, her students stop and pair up with the closest student. She then asks a question about her lesson and gives each pair the opportunity to discuss it. Once she feels that they have had adequate time to discuss, Ms. Paulk asks one pair, who she overheard having a rich discussion about the question, to share what they talked about with the rest of the class. She then starts the music again and the process starts over. Ms. Paulk found that with some classes she used three questions and others four, depending on the amount of time that each group needed to discuss each question.

Ms. Paulk chose to ask the questions orally, but it is also effective to post them on the board so that students can refer to them during their discussions.

Listening in on student discussions provides formative assessment and also allows the teacher to clarify, correct, and expand upon student responses, ensuring that all students take away the key information from the discussion.

Mingle to Music

Preparation: Music needs to be ready to play, and questions or prompts prepared.

Time Needed: 10–12 minutes

Grouping: Pairs

Procedures for Students:

1. When the music plays, mingle safely and silently throughout the classroom.

2. When the music stops, freeze and pair up with the person closest to you.

3. Listen for the question or discussion prompt.

4. Take turns discussing the question or prompt with your partner.

5. When the music resumes, begin mingling again and repeat process.

Suggested Adaptations and Applications to Other Content Areas:

- Instead of discussing a question or prompt, students can share something they have written or created.

(Continued)

(Continued)

- Questions or prompts can be given to students in advance so they have time to think about them and they can begin to construct their responses.

- If space is limited, half the students can mingle and pair up with a student who is seated. Then they switch places for the next round, so that the seated student has the opportunity to move.

- For question ideas for specific content areas, refer to Question Stems in Chapter 2.

Classroom Close-Up: Box-It

I use Box-It as guided practice for science and social studies concepts. For example, in science I have used it to practice how to read weather maps. I put questions in each box that ask students to analyze and interpret the different fronts on various weather maps and interpret the weather conditions that come with a particular front. In social studies when we were studying the causes of the American Revolution, I put the different acts in each box and asked them to explain everything they knew about the Stamp Act, Tea Act, Quartering Act, and so on. This allows the students to teach each other, while I facilitate the process. The Box-It instructional technique allows me, as the teacher, to see who I need to provide with additional instruction and who needs enrichment.

—Allison Boozer, fourth-grade teacher, Newberry, SC

BOX-IT

Ms. Paulk spends a lot of time designing lessons that will be engaging to her students. Terrance looks forward to her stories and video clips. Had she planned ahead to embed purposeful movement, Ms. Paulk would have had a strategy for reengaging her students before fatigue and decreased productivity hit. Box-It provides an effective structure for connecting movement to learning and has a variety of applications.

Text-Based Questions

If Ms. Paulk wanted her students to read and discuss a piece of text connected to her lesson, she could use Box-It as a strategy to structure a collaborative analysis of the text while providing purposeful movement. Ms. Paulk could create rich, text-based questions and plug them in to the Box-It template (see Resource 3). Students find a partner and are given a specified amount of time to work on the first question together. Once they have reread the part of the text referenced in the question, discussed it, and synthesized their discussion into a response they agree upon, both students write the answer in the appropriate box. They would then sign each other's Box-It sheets below their responses. This builds in a measure of accountability for students to work collaboratively and will allow Ms. Paulk to follow up with pairs as needed. When time is called, students find a new partner and work on the second question. This continues until all questions have been answered.

Vocabulary

Vocabulary terms are put into the boxes. Students pair up to use prior knowledge and provided resources to generate a definition for the words. Student definitions can then be discussed, compared to dictionary or glossary definitions, and expanded or refined.

Math

Math problems are put into the boxes (see Resource 4). Students pair up and choose a problem to "teach" a partner. One student will listen and provide assistance as the other student demonstrates and explains how to solve the problem. They then trade roles.

Music, Art, Physical Education

Skills to demonstrate are put into the boxes (e.g., draw a C on the staff; demonstrate and explain the correct form for a push-up; demonstrate and explain the difference between primary and secondary colors). Students pair up and choose a skill to demonstrate to a partner. One student will listen and provide feedback as the other student demonstrates and explains the skill. They then trade roles.

Box-It

Preparation: Box-It form (see Resource 3 or 4) needs to be populated with questions, problems, or tasks, and copies of the form need to be made for each student.

Time Needed: 10–30 minutes (based on number of boxes and how much time is given for each box)

Grouping: Pairs

Procedures for Students (Text-Based Questions):

1. Find a partner.
2. Read the first question on your Box-It sheet together.
3. Reread the part of the text referenced in the question.

(Continued)

(Continued)

4. Discuss the question.

5. Based on your discussion, synthesize a response to the question.

6. Write your response on your individual Box-It sheets.

7. Sign each other's Box-It sheets below that question.

8. When directed, find a new partner and repeat the process.

Procedures for Students (Vocabulary):

1. Find a partner.

2. Discuss the first vocabulary term on your Box-It sheet together.

3. Use provided resources to find out more about the term.

4. Based on your discussion and research, generate a definition for the term in your words.

5. Write your definitions on your individual Box-It sheets.

6. Sign each other's Box-It sheets below that term.

7. When directed, find a new partner and repeat the process.

8. Be prepared to discuss your definitions with the group.

Procedures for Students (Math):

1. Find a partner.

2. Student A chooses a problem from the Box-It sheet to teach Student B.

3. Student B listens and provides assistance as necessary.

4. Student B signs the appropriate box on Student A's Box-It sheet.

5. Students A and B trade roles.

6. When directed, find a new partner and repeat the process.

Procedures for Students (Physical Education, Art, Music, Etc.):

1. Find a partner.

2. Student A chooses a task from the Box-It sheet to demonstrate to Student B.

3. Student B listens and provides feedback.

4. Student B signs the appropriate box on Student A's Box-It sheet.

5. Students A and B trade roles.

6. When directed, find a new partner and repeat the process.

Suggested Adaptations:

- Instead of questions or math problems, very young students' boxes can have letters or numbers. Pairs of students can generate words that start with the letter and provide different ways to make the number.

- To differentiate for students who complete work at different rates, students do not have to be given the same amount of time to complete each box. Some students might finish all the boxes, while others only finish some of them.

- To provide intentional pairing of students, the teacher can have preplanned partners and post them between each box.

- A Box-It does not have to be completed in one block of time. It can be stopped at any point and resumed when time allows or when purposeful movement is needed.

QUIZ-QUIZ-TRADE

Ms. Paulk could use the Quiz-Quiz-Trade strategy (Kagan & Kagan, 2009) with her students as a meaningful way to create individualized understanding of the content presented in the video clip. Students would view the video (possibly two times depending on Ms. Paulk's goals for the lesson) and craft question/answer index cards related to the essential concepts. The students would write one question on the front of the index cards and the answer on the back. As students perform this task, Ms. Paulk could use this time to informally measure student understanding of the essential concepts she wanted them to grasp, and also assess how well they are able to create their own questions, an expectation of next-generation academic standards. Once students receive the "thumbs up" from

Classroom Close-Up:
Quiz-Quiz-Trade/Mingle to Music

In my kindergarten classroom, we use Quiz-Quiz-Trade mixed with Mingle to Music almost daily! My kids loved it when learning letters, numbers, sight words, shapes, and so on. They love mingling to the music around the classroom and especially love quizzing their friends with their cards. After my kids quiz each other on their cards and then they trade cards, each one has another opportunity to think about that card when he or she quizzes the next partner. I love this strategy because it gives me a purposeful way to use flashcards, and it mixes learning and assessment with movement.

—Jennifer Smallwood,
kindergarten teacher, Columbia, SC

her that they have crafted relevant questions and evidence-based answers, they stand up with their cards and randomly partner with classmates. Partners would take turns sharing their question, and the other partner would have to answer the question based on information from the viewed video clip. This process would continue until Ms. Paulk determined there had been adequate practice and her goals were met through the task. At this point, students are ready for Ms. Paulk's direct instruction to help them deepen the understanding they gained from playing Quiz-Quiz-Trade.

Quiz-Quiz-Trade can be used as a structure for introducing content or activating prior knowledge at the beginning of a lesson. It is also an effective strategy for introducing or reviewing vocabulary. During the guided practice portion of a lesson, Quiz-Quiz-Trade provides the opportunity for students to practice the content or skills they have been taught. It is also a way to provide meaningful closure to lessons to ensure students have the opportunity to reflect upon and process what they learned.

Posting procedures for Quiz-Quiz-Trade allows students to be more accountable for themselves and others, be more productive and self-disciplined, and allows the teacher to be more of a facilitator, rather than having to repeat instructions and verbally redirect students. When the teacher listens in as students quiz each other, she is able to do some formative assessment that will guide her next steps.

Quiz-Quiz-Trade

Preparation: No preparation is required if students create their own set of cards. If preparing the cards, it will require 15–20 minutes.

Time Needed: 8 – 10 minutes

Grouping: Pairs

Procedures for Older Students:

1. When directed, stand up with your card and find a learning partner not sitting near you.

2. Partner 1 shares the question on his or her card while Partner 2 determines the answer.

3. If Partner 2 does not know the answer, Partner 1 "coaches" Partner 2 to determine the answer.

4. Roles reverse and Partner 2 shares the question on his or her card while Partner 1 determines the answer.

5. Once both partners have shared their questions and answered them, they trade cards and play continues until time is called by the teacher.

Procedures for Younger Students:

1. Walk with card.

2. Freeze.

3. Face a friend.

4. Quiz each other.

5. Trade cards.

6. Hand up and repeat until time is called.

Suggested Adaptations:

- Have pre-developed Quiz-Quiz-Trade cards readily available for younger students.

- Replace words with pictures for very young learners.

- If there is very limited space to move, students can stand and participate with the person in front, behind, diagonally, beside, etc.

Source: This material has been adapted with permission from Kagan Publishing & Professional Development from the following book: Kagan, Spencer, & Kagan, Miguel. *Kagan Cooperative Learning*. San Clemente, CA: Kagan Publishing, 2009. 1 (800) 933-2667. www.KaganOnline.com.

KINESTHETIC MAPPING

Ms. Paulk really wants students to remember three key ideas from her lesson, so, as usual, she asked them to write them in their notebooks. Ms. Paulk's biggest frustration is one that is also shared by her colleagues: how to get the information out of their notebooks and into their brains. Kinesthetic mapping is a powerful way to make this happen.

Kinesthetic mapping is the process of creating body movements to represent terms, concepts, or ideas. This creates a non-linguistic representation of the concept, and according to the meta-analysis of research published in *Classroom Instruction That Works*, "the more we use both systems of representation—linguistic and non-linguistic—the better we are able to think about and recall knowledge" (Dean, Hubbell, Pitler, & Stone, 2013).

Ms. Paulk created a simple movement for each key idea and taught them to her students. They practiced them until they could do them automatically. Each time Ms. Paulk referred to one of the key ideas, she did the movement for it and asked the students to do the same. The next day, she found that when asked to recall the three key ideas, instead of reading from their notebooks, the students used their kinesthetic map. They had done it! The key ideas were out of their notebooks and into their brains!

Kinesthetic mapping is not a game of charades. It is a meaningful and memorable movement that represents the term or idea and makes something conceptual more tangible and concrete. It should also recall to mind more about the concept than just the words. In order for it to be a truly effective non-linguistic representation, it must "elaborate on knowledge" (Dean et al., 2013) and extend student thinking about the concept.

Kinesthetic mapping not only provides purposeful movement, it also allows students to store information in their bodies through movements that are readily available to them anytime and anywhere, even when their notes or textbooks are not.

Kinesthetic Mapping

Preparation: Meaningful body movements for each term, idea, or concept should be prepared in advance

Time Needed: 5–10 minutes

Grouping: No grouping is needed

Procedures for Students:

1. Watch the kinesthetic map demonstrated by your teacher.

2. Practice it with a partner.

3. Each time you, your teacher, or another student refers to the concept(s) you have mapped, perform the body movement.

Suggested Adaptations and Applications to Other Content Areas:

- Individuals, pairs, or groups of students can develop kinesthetic maps for terms or concepts and teach them and explain their significance to the rest of the class.

- Students can pair up and quiz each other on concepts using kinesthetic mapping.

- Suggested uses for English language arts: parts of a letter, vocabulary terms

- Suggested uses for mathematics: types of lines and angles; order of operations

- Suggested uses for science: parts of a cell; states of matter; water cycle

- Suggested uses for social studies: landforms; lines of latitude/longitude; location of continents and oceans

- Suggested uses for physical education/music/art: position of notes on a staff

GO TO YOUR CORNER

Ms. Paulk wanted her students to process and reflect upon the three key ideas from the lesson. Go to Your Corner is an effective strategy to facilitate this process while embedding purposeful movement. Ms. Paulk wrote her three key ideas on chart paper and posted them in three corners of the classroom. She then asked the students to decide which of the three key ideas they felt they understood best and to go stand in that corner. Each group huddled up to discuss their key idea. Ms. Paulk visited each group and listened in on their discussion to ensure accuracy and extend thinking. She then formed new groups with members from each corner and asked them to take turns sharing with the others in their new group what they knew about their key idea. When they returned to their seats, every single student had processed and discussed the three key points of the lesson with their peers.

Go to Your Corner involves a decision or a choice. This makes the strategy not only physically engaging, but also mentally and emotionally engaging for students. Teachers can post characters from a novel and ask students to choose the character they identify with most (or least); they can post quotes from historical figures and ask students to choose the quote that impacts them most and to explain why; they can post a variety of math problems and ask students to choose the one that is the easiest or most difficult and to explain it to another student. Ms. Paulk had three corners, but a teacher could have more or less depending on the number of choices the students are given. Anything that involves a choice or asks students to form an opinion is ideal for Go to Your Corner.

Classroom Close-up:
Go to Your Corner

I have used Go to Your Corner so many times that I really can't imagine kindergarten without it! There are so many ways to use it. One way is to post names of characters from our story in corners of the room. Students think about which character is their favorite and why. They "go to their corner" and group up with one or two other students who went to the same corner. They then discuss why this character is their favorite. This is such a wonderful way to get children to talk and share when maybe they wouldn't be the ones who raise their hands in class to say something. It is also a perfect opportunity for me to "listen in" on their conversations. I also noticed how it allowed students to pair up with peers they may not know too well. It's a building-community time like no other! Kindergarteners love to move and talk . . . what better way than to put Go to Your Corner in place!
—Tina Jackson, kindergarten teacher, Blythewood, SC

Go to Your Corner

Preparation: Prompts need to be written and posted in the "corners" where students will stand

Time Needed: 10–12 minutes

Grouping: Small groups (varies based on number of choices and how many students choose each)

Procedures for Students:

1. Think about the statements or pictures posted in the room and listen to your teacher's direction.

2. Go to the corner and stand beneath the poster that best fits.

3. Huddle up with the other students in your corner and discuss.

4. When directed, form a new group with students from the other corners.

5. Take turns sharing what you know about your topic or prompt.

6. Return to your seat when finished.

Suggested Adaptations and Applications to Other Content Areas:

- If groups in a corner are too large, students can cluster into smaller groups within the group for discussion.

- If there are corners with no students, teachers can stop and process why no one went to that corner. Depending on the prompt, it might indicate that reteaching is needed.

- To add movement to multiple choice questions, post A, B, C, and D in the four corners of the room. Ask students to go to the corner of the room that matches the correct answer and explain to a partner how they knew it was correct. Students who went to the wrong corner can explain why they thought that answer was correct and a student from the correct corner can help them understand how to get the correct answer.

MOTIONLESS MODELS

As students came into Ms. Paulk's classroom, she could have immediately engaged them in the day's lesson by implementing the Motionless Models strategy. On the board, Ms. Paulk could have listed the six critical academic vocabulary terms students would need to analyze to deepen understanding of today's close reading. As students entered her class, they would be given one of these words. They would find other students who have the same vocabulary term and then follow the written procedures for Motionless Models. As small groups of students (three or four per group) read and analyze the word, they must develop a frozen scene or pose that captures its essence.

While in this scene or pose, all students are communicating and contributing to capture the word's meaning so it is a complete and comprehensive representation.

Motionless Models allow students to create physical poses, gestures, and facial expressions that demonstrate comprehension and create more in-depth critical-thinking skills rather than using the more "traditional" mode of learning through words. This collaborative strategy is appealing to kinesthetic learners and allows all students to be creative while strengthening their comprehension of varied concepts and skills.

Motionless Models can be used with any concept or skill that requires students to focus their attention and freeze their bodies and faces to show action in order to develop a scene, picture, or series of scenes or pictures to bring the concepts and skills "to life." Their expressive faces, body poses, and how they pose in relationship to one another creates a living picture or sculpture. In its simplest form students simply freeze to capture a moment in time. Teachers can apply this strategy to history, literature, science, math, physical education, band, and any other academic and arts-related task and it can be used with all ages.

In the process of creating Motionless Models, students are involved in developing their senses, building and activating background knowledge, asking questions, determining what is important, making inferences, and synthesizing information that will help them best capture the information.

Motionless Models

Preparation: Determine ahead of time what academic concept or skill you will want students to analyze and prepare materials as needed.

Time Needed: 8–10 minutes

Grouping: Individuals, pairs, triads, groups of 4

Procedures for Students:

1. Brainstorm ways to demonstrate the learning task.

2. Come to consensus as to the most effective way to do this.

3. Practice with your group.

4. When time is called, perform your Motionless Model for others.

(Continued)

(Continued)

Suggested Applications to Other Content Areas:

- Suggested uses for English language arts: create a motionless model that communicates mood or specific themes

- Suggested uses for mathematics: visual representations of the operations; various geometric shapes

- Suggested uses for science: motionless model of life cycles; motionless model of a chemical reaction

- Suggestion uses for social studies: scenes from history; representations of each branch and/or level of government

- Suggested uses for physical education/music/art: motionless models that represent domain-specific vocabulary terms

Questions for Reflection

1. For a week, keep a journal to document how often your students move during a class period.

   - How much of this movement was planned by you and connected to their learning?
   - How often did they create their own movement (getting up to throw away trash, going to the bathroom/nurse/pencil sharpener, etc.)?
   - Based on this data, create a plan for ensuring that movement is frequent and purposeful.

2. Before you begin teaching, set a timer for 10 minutes. When the timer goes off, stop your instruction and implement a purposeful movement strategy that will allow your students to process the content that you have taught.

   - What did you notice about your students' attention/focus/energy level after you implemented the movement strategy?
   - What challenges did you encounter, and how will you address these next time you use this structure?

6 Make It Stick

*Powerful Strategies for Closing a
Lesson and Providing Reflection*

VIGNETTES

A Teacher's Perspective

Casey Hart was thrilled with the progress her students had made the previous day learning the attributes of two-dimensional shapes. She had a great shape scavenger hunt planned for today and couldn't wait to get started. She began by activating prior knowledge only to discover that her students remembered nothing from the previous day! She looked out at their blank stares and confused expressions and wanted to cry. "Well, I guess we will just start from scratch," she sighed.

A Student's Perspective

Noah sat patiently on the carpet. He hoped that Ms. Hart would talk about what they did yesterday. He loved sorting things. He made his piles very neat and organized, and she had commented on that yesterday. Right now she is talking about something else, so he would just wait until they talked about sorting.

WHAT IS CLOSURE?

We have all experienced Ms. Hart's frustration: we taught it, but they forgot it! Noah remembered what he *did* in Ms. Hart's class; he just didn't remember what he *learned*. To get off the hamster wheel of "teach it–they forget it–so reteach it," provide effective closure to each lesson.

Closure is the process of wrapping up the lesson and providing an opportunity for students to summarize what they learned. As the teacher listens in to students' learning summaries, any confusion or misconceptions can be clarified, allowing students to leave the lesson with clear and correct information about what was learned. Closure not only provides informal assessment data to the teacher, closure allows the students the opportunity to assess their own understanding and set goals for their learning.

Ms. Hart had her students involved in a meaningful learning task: sorting shapes by attributes. Once the students had the experience of sorting the shapes, Ms. Hart could have asked the students to explain to a friend how they sorted the shapes. Then she could have asked them to think about and share what they now understand about shapes. Students leave the lesson having articulated what they *learned*: that shapes have different attributes, not just with the experience of putting shapes into neat, well-organized piles.

This chapter contains eight strategies to use to close lessons and provide reflection.

WHY IT WORKS

Have you ever sat down at Starbucks with your best friend and started talking about everything under the sun? Later, when you are shopping or when you have gotten home, you find yourself reflecting on the conversation and saying things like "I wish I had told her about . . .," or "I should have thought about . . .," or "why didn't I think to tell her . . ." As human beings, all of us have these moments because our brains are designed to do so. The term "let it marinate" is often used when talking about reflection and closure (Block, 2014) because a defining condition of being human is that we have to mentally wander through where we have been and to try to make sense of our experiences and our learning. When our brains link and construct meaning, insight and complex learning are enhanced, which equips students to be problem solvers, critical thinkers, and goal-setters of the 21st century.

School is generally not structured in a way that easily accommodates reflection and closure because of one four-letter word: time. The end of a class period may often feel rushed, therefore, eliminating this critical component of effective lesson design. An alternate view could be to use these last moments as a time for students to articulate their final thoughts and ideas and process their experiences. According to Dr. Judy Willis

Classroom Close-up:
Why I Use Closure

I struggled with closure for over a year. I didn't want to spend all the time that I thought it would take, and I really didn't see any real need for it. Once I looked at the research and realized how important closure is, I decided to start doing it. I made sure it was on the board every day as part of our agenda, so I would not forget.

I now do some sort of closure for every lesson, and I have seen great results. Last year, I consistently made time for some sort of closure and my state test results were much better than any other year.

One closure technique I like to use, which doesn't take a lot of time, is 3-2-1. By incorporating this at the end of my lesson, it allows for two things: (1) for me to know and gauge where my students are, and to see the understandings and misunderstandings, and (2) for the students to process what they learned and realize what they still have questions about. Sometimes they do this in writing, while other times they do it verbally with a partner. If a student can articulate and explain what he or she knows or learned, it reinforces the concept. By mixing up the writing and verbal, it also keeps the interest alive in the students. When students discuss their 3-2-1 with a partner, it creates opportunities for the partner to ask any questions and clarify anything fuzzy.

—Marsha Neal, sixth-grade math teacher, Hardeeville, SC

(2013), "processing time, reflection time, and metacognition are vital to the learning environment. Thus, much of the effort put into teaching and studying is wasted because students do not adequately process their experiences, nor are they given time to reflect upon them." This does not have to involve a lot of time. According to the article "The Impact of Group Processing on Achievement in Cooperative Learning Groups" (Yager, Johnson, Johnson, & Snider, 1986), spending five minutes at the end of a class period reflecting upon what was learned and setting goals for improvement led not only to increased achievement, but also increased retention of information.

STRATEGIES FOR CLOSURE

INPUT, OUTPUT

Input, Output is an effective strategy because it stimulates student thinking as they reflect on an essential question or search for evidence in response to a prompt at the end of lessons. It creates high levels of active participation because students want to get up out of their seats and they want to socialize, and it allows them to engage in structured academic discussions that are nonthreatening and safe.

Casey Hart should consider using this strategy at the end of her lessons as a way for students to reflect on what they have learned, as well as what they have gained from their classmates during the learning process. She could teach her lesson and then ask students to participate in Input, Output. Her students would reflect on the essential question and learning target for the day's lesson by having think time. Suppose Ms. Hart had asked the question, "What are five things you noticed about your shapes?" Students would think about the learning task they just completed about sorting shapes into different attributes. Then they would record five things noticed in the "Output" column of their T-Charts. Now they are equipped to share with their classmates, and to both give and receive information to deepen understanding of the content.

Once her students were ready, they would stand up and find partners, with one peer being Student A and one being Student B. Student A would ask Student B to share one thing learned during the lesson, and Student A would record it on his or her own T-Chart under the column "Input" because the information is being received from Student B. Then Student A would give Student B information from his or her output column, and Student B would record it under the "Input" column (see below). Once they have each given and received one idea, they find new partners and the process is repeated. This continues until the teacher calls time or students have given all of their ideas away.

Use of this strategy would help students like Noah solidify and cement their own understanding about the day's content because they would have to think critically about it before moving on to another subject or task.

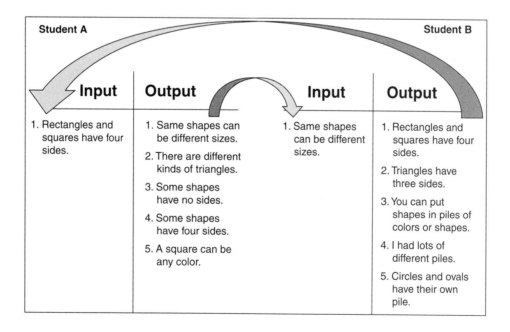

Input, Output

Preparation: Have Input, Output T-Charts readily available; model and practice how this strategy should look, sound, and feel like when being implemented productively.

Time Needed: 5–10 minutes depending on the age and closure task

Grouping: Individuals

Procedures for Students:

1. Think about the question or prompt given.

2. Record your thinking into the Output column on your T-Chart.

3. When directed, find a partner.

4. Share one of your ideas and tell your partner to record it under his or her Input column.

5. Ask your partner to share an idea.

6. Record the idea into the Input column of your T-Chart.

7. Find a new partner and repeat the process.

8. Continue until you have given away all of your ideas and you have received enough ideas to complete your Input column.

Suggested Adaptations:

- Younger students and special needs students could do this task orally instead of putting into a T-Chart.

- The number of ideas recorded could vary from task to task.

GOAL-SETTING

On May 25, 1961, President John F. Kennedy announced a goal: America would put a person safely on the moon before the end of the decade. Many thought this was impossible. To people's amazement, Kennedy's ambitious goal was achieved on July 20, 1969, when Neil Armstrong stepped onto the Moon's surface. In this context, JFK's initial goal-setting guided and motivated Armstrong's giant step for mankind. Goals are not only in the domain of leaders, though. They are part of our everyday lives.

The process of setting goals allows students to choose where they want to go in school and what they want to achieve. By knowing what they want to achieve, they know what they have to concentrate on and improve. Having clearly defined goals, which students can measure, will allow them to take pride in accomplishing those goals. They can see clear forward progress in what might have seemed like a long, drawn-out process.

By setting goals students can:

1. Improve their academic performance

2. Increase their motivation to achieve

3. Increase pride and satisfaction in performance

4. Improve their self-confidence

By setting goals and measuring their achievements, students are able to see what they have done and what they are capable of. Seeing their results gives the confidence and assurance that they need to believe they can achieve higher goals.

One way Ms. Hart could implement the goal-setting process in her classroom would be by letting students take adequate time at the end of her lesson to reflect on their current understanding of the attributes of two-dimensional shapes. In her kindergarten classroom, the goal-setting process would look somewhat different based on time of year and ability levels (see image on page 116).

Once students develop a mental program for what it looks, sounds, and feels like when setting personalized learning goals, Casey's students would soon realize how fun, exciting, and meaningful the goal-setting process is and how they have the choice and can control the outcomes of those goals—thus making the learning process more intentional and meaningful for *all* students.

Goal-Setting

Preparation: Make sure you leave enough time at the end of the lesson for students to reflect on that day's learning before they begin the goal-setting process. (See Resources for template.)

Time Needed: 5–8 minutes (depending on grade level and goals to be determined)

Grouping: Individuals, pairs, small groups, or whole group

Procedures for Students:

1. Think about what we learned today.

2. What part of it did you struggle to understand or want to do better?

3. Create a goal to meet this need.

(Continued)

(Continued)

My Reading Goal:	☐ **Accomplished** ☐ **Still Improving**
My Math Goal:	☐ **Accomplished** ☐ **Still Improving**
My Writing Goal:	☐ **Accomplished** ☐ **Still Improving**

4. Record your goal.

5. Participate in a Group Huddle to tell how you will work on the goal you determined.

6. Meet with your teacher to discuss.

Suggested Adaptations:

- Primary grades will need lots of modeling and scaffolding opportunities so they can be gradually released to set their own learning goals.

Beginning with a class goal based on formative assessment results is an effective way to start the process and move gradually into goal-setting conferences followed by students setting their own individualized goals.

- Older students may need more quality time to develop their goals.
- Students on block schedules may want to set one goal for the week in that specific class instead of creating goals each class period.
- All goals do not have to be written; they can be shared orally and then reflected upon over a period of time.

STATEMENTS OF INSIGHT

Noah's insight following the shape-sorting task was that his piles were neat and well-organized. Ms. Hart could provide a structure for developing a statement of insight to guide Noah's thinking back to the learning objective for this task, rather than the task itself. An effective way to ensure that these statements reflect what was learned is to provide sentence stems to frame student thinking. "Now I understand that shapes _____" leads students to think about shapes, not about sorting into piles. As Noah is sharing his statement of insight with a friend, if Ms. Hart hears him say, "Now I understand that shapes can be put into piles" she can extend his thinking with further questions, asking him to think about how he put them into piles, what the shapes in each pile have in common, and so on. At this point, Ms. Hart can bring the students back together to share their statements of insight. As she captures the insights on the board, students are able to see how much they learned about shapes today.

Classroom Close-Up:
Statements of Insight/Exit Tickets

The Statements of Insight strategy is one of my favorite ways to reflect after a lesson, field trip, or experience because it provides me with a deeper understanding of my students. Because I want student reflection to be deep, and for my middle schoolers to be transparent in their responses, I know there has to be a safe, nurturing, emotional environment built on mutual respect in place first. When this culture has been established, Statements of Insight becomes part of our daily closure routine. Students think about what they learned or discovered from the lesson or experience and express it using "Today I learned _____" or "Now I understand _____." Sometimes they share this with a shoulder partner; other times they write it down and it is their exit ticket. Walking around and listening to these reflections provides insight for me, and it also provides an opportunity for me to stop and add my own reflections.

—Marsha Weddington, sixth-grade ELA/Social Studies teacher, Tulsa, OK

Statements of Insight

Preparation: Prepare sentence frames that will take students back to the learning objective.

Time Needed: 5 minutes

Grouping: Flexible (pairs, threes, or fours)

Procedures for Students:

1. Think about what you learned today when we (insert task) _____.

2. Use this sentence stem to frame your thinking: Now I understand _____.

3. Make sure your sentence reflects what you *learned*, not what you *did*.

4. Share your Statement of Insight with a partner.

5. Listen reflectively as your partner shares.

6. Be prepared to share your insights with the class.

Suggested Adaptations:

- Statements of Insight can also be written.
- Students can share Statements of Insight in small groups of three or four and combine their insights into a comprehensive statement.

FIST TO FIVE

Ms. Hart was frustrated and felt defeated because she thought her students were really "getting it," but when she asked questions about the previous day's learning her students disappointed her and she was disappointed in herself. What was she missing? Why did her students not understand? How should she proceed so they did get it?

Another effective strategy Ms. Hart could have implemented for closing her lesson and for providing reflection is called Fist to Five. Fist to Five provides an opportunity for all students in a class to indicate when they do not understand a concept, procedure, or set of directions and need additional support for their learning. It is especially effective with individual students who are reluctant to let the teacher know that they are experiencing difficulty during a lesson. It encourages metacognition by raising self-awareness of how ready students feel to proceed with their learning.

It allows the teacher to direct the challenge and pace of lessons toward the needs of the students rather than following a prescribed instructional plan. The quick read of the class provides teachers with the feedback they need to modify the lesson or pair students up to help each other.

At the end of her lesson, Ms. Hart could have asked her students to rate their level of understanding based on their knowledge about the attributes of two-dimensional shapes—students would hold up one finger to show they do not understand at all, hold up two fingers to show they need to go over the information presented again, hold up three fingers to show they think they get it but aren't sure, hold up four fingers to show they get it and hold up five fingers to show they can explain it to others. Once Ms. Hart does a quick scan of her class, she could quickly adjust her lesson for the next day to ensure it's more intentional and meets the needs of her students effectively so students make the connection between prior learning and present learning.

Fist to Five

Preparation: No preparation is needed if the procedure has already been introduced and practiced consistently over time.

Time Needed: 1–3 minutes

Grouping: Individualized

Procedures for Students:

1. Think about what you have learned about _____.

2. Rate your level of understanding using Fist to 5.

3. When asked, hold up the appropriate finger(s).

4. Share with a partner why you chose that level.

Suggested Adaptations:

This strategy could be modified to a three-finger strategy: one finger means "I don't get it," two fingers means "I partially get it," and three fingers means "I get it."

ONE-WORD SUMMARIES

The purpose of closure is to allow students to summarize their learning—to take everything they were taught and experienced during the lesson and "put it in a nutshell." This nutshell can be one word.

To help students avoid the obvious, they can be given off-limit words. For example, Ms. Hart could ask students to come up with one word to explain what they learned about shapes, but they cannot use the following words: shape, circle, square, triangle, rectangle, or oval. Now students have to dig deeper and think more critically to think of a word to summarize what was learned. Noah comes up with the word "alike" and explains to his partner that all the shapes in each pile are alike in some way and begins to describe how they are alike. Ms. Hart listens to the words different students come up with and has two or three students share their thinking so that students hear different perspectives on the same content. Ms. Hart can then begin the next day's lesson with those words.

One-Word Summaries

Preparation: No preparation is needed.

Time Needed: 5 minutes

Grouping: Pairs

Procedures for Students:

1. Think about what your learned today and put it into one word.
2. The following words are off-limits: _____
3. Tell your word to a partner and explain why you chose that word.
4. Listen reflectively as your partner explains his or her word.
5. Be prepared to share your words and your thinking with the class.

Suggested Adaptations:

There are no adaptations needed for this strategy.

ON YOUR MARK

Casey Hart felt like all of us as teachers have felt at one time (or many) in our teaching careers. You teach a great lesson. Students are engaged. Students are excited. You feel like a rock star! But then during your opening of the next day's lesson, students stare at you like deer in headlights! You feel defeated! You feel frustrated. How could students seem so knowledgeable about a lesson one day and then know nothing the next?

Implementing a structure that helps students recap the day's learning can eliminate this all too common scenario. On Your Mark is a strategy that offers an alternative to the traditional "teacher asks a question, students raise hands to respond" structure in which the teacher then calls on one student to answer during reflection and closure of a lesson. In On Your Mark, each student is given a colored index card with a colored dot sticker. This is the student's "mark." Students form groups with students with the same color index card. Once the groups are formed, the teacher poses a question about the lesson's content, asks students to stand and get in a Group Huddle (see Chapter 2, under Simultaneous Response Techniques) to discuss, come to a consensus for a group answer, and then sit down. This gives the teacher a nonverbal cue that everyone is ready to continue. The teacher has a stack of colored index cards that match the colors given to the students. She randomly pulls one from the stack. She also has a cup or envelope filled with colored dots that match those on the students' cards. She then pulls one of those. The student(s) in the class who have the same color card that was pulled with the color of the dot that was pulled is "on the mark" and will share a summary of what his or her group discussed. This strategy gives confidence to struggling students because they know they will have a meaningful answer to give the class. It also provides the rich academic discussion that is needed in our classrooms to ensure academic language and assists in developing deeper understanding of content.

The information shared by collaborative groups also gives teachers accurate feedback on what students' takeaways were from the lesson in order to reflect on goals and objectives for the next lesson, which would eliminate how Ms. Hart felt during her math lesson, as well as Noah.

After the two-dimensional shapes sorting lesson was completed, Ms. Hart could have implemented On Your Mark as an effective closure strategy. She could have asked her kindergarten class, "How would you explain two-dimensional shapes to someone struggling with them?" Her students would get into a Group Huddle, come up with a meaningful answer together, and be prepared to share their answer if called on. Noah would have loved participating in On Your Mark because it would have given him an opportunity to cement his understanding of the day's lesson in order to make sense of what was being introduced the following day. He wouldn't have mentally checked out as he waited for his teacher to talk about what they did the day before because he had an opportunity to reflect on and effectively close the previous day's learning.

On Your Mark

Preparation: Count out the number of each color index card to match the number of students you want in a group and put a different colored dot on

(Continued)

(Continued)

each card; prepare questions that ask students to analyze and synthesize to ensure quality academic discussion in small groups.

Time Needed: 5–6 minutes

Grouping: 3–4 students per group

Procedures for Students:

1. Take a card.

2. Think about the question given.

3. Participate in a Group Huddle to discuss with your collaborative group.

4. Sit down when all of you have shared.

5. The teacher will pull a colored card to determine which group will share and pull a colored dot to determine which student within that chosen group will share what was discussed.

Suggested Adaptation:

- Some students may want to jot notes as their group discusses the question so that they will feel more prepared if their mark is chosen.

EXIT TICKETS

Ms. Hart was both surprised and disappointed when she realized that her students didn't remember what she had taught them about the attributes of shapes. She needed a snapshot of what students were thinking as they left the lesson, so that she would know how to start her lesson the next day. Exit tickets provide that snapshot.

An exit ticket is a "ticket out the door" as students leave one lesson and transition to something else (a new lesson, lunch, another class, dismissal). They allow the teacher to get a glimpse into the students' thinking and provide effective formative assessment. The ticket can be a response to a question, a summary of what was learned, or a solution to a problem. This can be written, drawn, or spoken and is given to the teacher during the transition time. The goal is that before students leave this learning experience and transition to something else, they have had the opportunity to think about what was learned so that they can let that learning "marinate."

After her students finished sorting their shapes, Ms. Hart could ask them to select two shapes from one of their piles and think about why they put them there. As they transition to center time, each student gives their shapes to Ms. Hart and briefly explains why they put them in the same pile. This is their exit ticket to go to centers.

Exit Tickets

Preparation: Prepare a question, problem, or task that will allow students to summarize their learning; if desired, you can create a physical ticket for students to complete.

Time Needed: 5 minutes

Grouping: Individuals

Procedures for Students:

1. Think about what you learned today.

2. Complete the statement, Today I learned _____ by _____.

3. Write your statement on a sticky note.

4. Post it on the door as you exit the classroom.

Suggested Adaptations:

- After students prepare their exit tickets they can meet in pairs to compare learning and add to, refine, and extend their responses before exiting.

- Exit tickets can be brief statements spoken to the teacher, symbols or illustrations to explain learning, or math problems students have solved.

3-2-1

The 3-2-1 strategy provides a structure for students to record their own personal understanding and summarize their learning as part of lesson closure and reflection. It provides an easy way for teachers to check for understanding by giving them the opportunity to identify areas that need reteaching and to gauge students' interest in a topic because they are thinking critically and independently as they answer the questions.

Ms. Hart could have used this strategy as part of her lesson closure and reflection to help Noah and her other students make the connection between what was learned on Day 1 with what is going to be learned on Day 2. She wanted them to have a clear understanding of two-dimensional shapes and their distinct attributes. Her 3-2-1 questions could be the following:

3 characteristics of two-dimensional shapes

2 examples of two-dimensional shapes

1 question you have about two-dimensional shapes

Her students would respond to the three prompts, orally or in written form. Ms. Hart could either read student responses or have a class discussion about the prompts that would then help her have a clear understanding of where to begin on Day 2. Everyone would win. Ms. Hart would feel much differently about beginning Day 2's lesson because her students would be responding differently to her questions, and Noah would feel much more connected to Day 2's lesson, as would all of Ms. Hart's students.

3-2-1

Preparation: Choose the topics for reflection ahead of time.

Time Needed: 5–7 minutes

Grouping: Individualized

Procedures for Students:

1. Read the questions associated with each number.

2. Think about your answers.

3. Write your responses on a sticky note, index card, sheet of paper, in your journal, or elsewhere.

4. Share with a partner when time is called.

Suggested Adaptations and Applications to Other Content Areas:

- Younger students could draw or respond orally to the questions being asked.

- Suggested uses in English language arts: 3 facts you found in the article, 2 opinions you have about the topic, 1 thing that inspired your thinking

- Suggested uses in mathematics: 3 strategies that can be used to solve these problems, 2 statements explaining why you chose the strategy you used, 1 misconception that you or someone else might have

- Suggested uses in science: 3 words that capture the main points we learned today, 2 questions you think might be on a test about this content, 1 visual representation to illustrate your understanding of what we learned

- Suggested uses in social studies: 3 ways these two events/people/concepts are different, 2 things they have in common, 1 symbol that represents each one

- Suggested uses in physical education/music/art: 3 things you noticed about _____, 2 things you wonder about _____, 1 thing you discovered about _____

Questions for Reflection

1. After reading this chapter, how has your thinking about closure changed?
2. Analyze your lessons for the week.

   - Have you planned for closure at the end of every lesson?
   - What strategy(ies) can you implement that will enhance the quality of your closure?

3. Using strategies from this chapter, plan for closure following each lesson for two weeks. At the end of the two weeks, do the following:

   - Think about any impact you have seen (academic, social, emotional) as a result of implementing closure consistently.
   - Survey your students to determine any impact they have experienced.

Resources

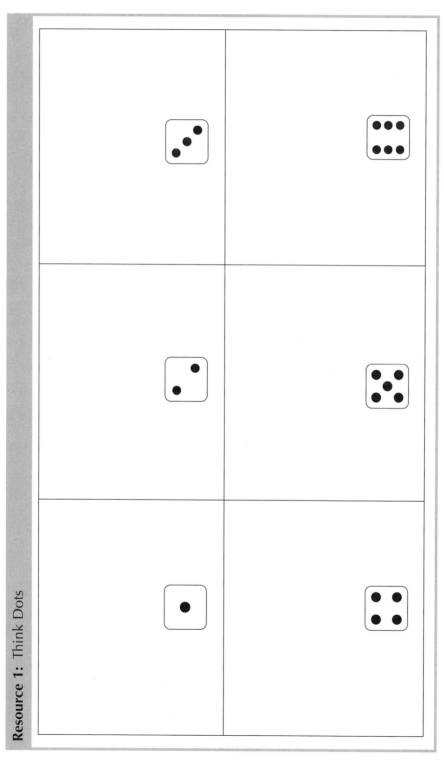

Clock Appointments

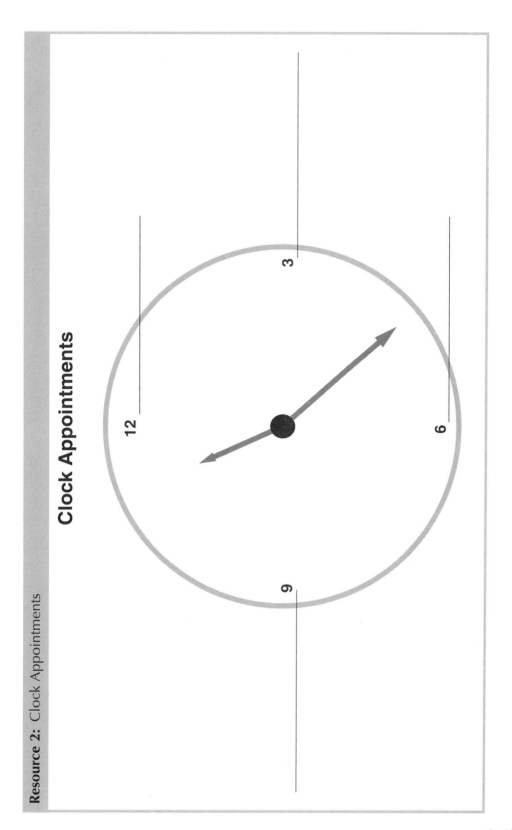

BOX-IT

BOX-IT

1.	2.	3.
4.	5.	6.

My Reading Goal:

☐   **Accomplished**

☐   **Still Improving**

My Math Goal:

☐   **Accomplished**

☐   **Still Improving**

My Writing Goal:

☐   **Accomplished**

☐   **Still Improving**

References

CHAPTER 1

Beyoncé, Dent, A., & Knowles, M. (2001). Survivor [Recorded by Destiny's Child]. On *Survivor* [CD]. New York, NY: Columbia Records.

Boyd, C., & Maal, N. (2008). *Soundtracks for learning: Using music in the classroom.* Bellingham, WA: LifeSounds Educational Services.

Dean, C. B., Hubbell, E. R., Pitler, H., & Stone, Bj. (2012). *Classroom instruction that works: Research-based strategies for increasing student achievement.* Alexandria, VA: ASCD.

LeDoux, J. (1998). *The emotional brain: The mysterious underpinnings of emotional life.* New York, NY: Simon & Schuster.

Reavis, G. H. (1999). *The animal school: The administration of the school curriculum with references to individual differences.* Peterborough, NH: Crystal Springs Books.

Sprenger, M. (2005). *How to teach so students remember.* Alexandria, VA: ASCD.

Wilson, J. W. (2015, December 5). "Cracking the learning code." *Cracking the Learning Code,* http://crackingthelearningcode.com/.

Wolfe, P. (2010). *Brain matters: Translating research into classroom practice* (2nd ed.) Alexandria, VA: ASCD.

CHAPTER 2

Chin, C. (2007). "Teacher questioning in science classrooms: Approaches that stimulate productive thinking." *Journal of Research for Science Teaching, 44*(6), 815–843.

Rowe, M. B. (1986). "Wait time: Slowing down may be a way of speeding up!" *Journal of Teacher Education, 37*(1), 43–50.

Vogler, K. E. (2008). "Asking good questions." *Educational Leadership, 65.* http://www.ascd.org/publications/educational-leadership/summer08/vol65/num09/Asking-Good-Questions.aspx.

Wagner, T. (2008). *The global achievement gap: Why even our best schools don't teach the new survival skills our children need—and what we can do about it.* New York, NY: Basic Books.

CHAPTER 3

Cazden, C. B. (2011). *Classroom discourse: The language of teaching and learning.* Portsmouth, NH: Heinemann.

Kotsopoulos, D. (2007). "It's like hearing a foreign language!" *The Mathematics Teacher, 101*(4), 301–305.

O'Connor, C. (n.d.). "Academically productive talk." *Word Generation,* Strategic Education Research Partnership, Boston University, http://wordgen.serpmedia .org/academic_vocabulary-and-apt.html.

CHAPTER 4

Aronson, E., Blaney, N., Stephin, C., Sikes, J., & Snapp, M. (1978). *The jigsaw classroom.* Beverly Hills, CA: Sage.

Aronson, E., & Patnoe, S. (2011). *Cooperation in the classroom: The jigsaw method* (3rd ed.). London: Pinter & Martin.

Johnson, D. W., & Johnson, R. T. (2009). "An educational psychology success story: Social interdependence theory and cooperative learning." *Journal of Educational Researcher, 38*(5), 365–379.

Kagan, S., & Kagan, M. *Kagan cooperative learning.* San Clemente, CA: Kagan Publishing, 2009.

Wagner, T. (2008). *The global achievement gap: Why even our best schools don't teach the new survival skills our children need and what we can do about it.* New York, NY: Basic Books.

CHAPTER 5

Cranz, G. (2000). *The chair: Rethinking culture, body, and design.* New York, NY: W. W. Norton & Company.

Dean, C. B., Hubbell, E. R., Pitler, H., & Stone, B. J. (2013). *Classroom instruction that works: Research based strategies for increasing student achievement* (2nd ed.). Alexandria, VA: ASCD.

Hannaford, C. (2007). *Smart moves: Why learning is not all in your head* (2nd ed.). Salt Lake City, UT: Great River Books.

Kagan, S., & Kagan, M. (2009). *Kagan cooperative learning.* San Clemente, CA: Kagan Publishing.

Ratey, J. (2002). *A user's guide to the brain: Perception attention, and the four theaters of the brain.* New York, NY: Knopf Doubleday.

Ratey, J. (2008). *Spark: The revolutionary new science of exercise and the brain.* New York, NY: Little, Brown and Company.

CHAPTER 6

Block, J. (2014, May 20). "Let it marinate: The importance of reflection and closing." *Edutopia,* http://www.edutopia.org/blog/let-it-marinate-reflection-closing-joshua-block.

Willis, J. (2013, August 3). "Why the brain benefits from reflection in learning," http://www.radteach.com/.

Yager, S., Johnson, R. T., Johnson, D. W., & Snider, B. (1986). "The impact of group processing on achievement in cooperative learning groups." *The Journal of Social Psychology, 126*(3), 389–398.

Index

CORWIN

A SAGE Publishing Company

CORWIN HAS ONE MISSION: to enhance education through intentional professional learning. We build long-term relationships with our authors, educators, clients, and associations who partner with us to develop and continuously improve the best evidence-based practices that establish and support lifelong learning.